Mom's Best Desserts

100 classic treats that taste as good now
as they did then

ANDREA CHESMAN & FRAN RABOFF

STOREY
BOOKS

Edited by Dianne M. Cutillo and Carey L. Boucher
Cover design and art direction by Meredith Maker
Cover photograph by Giles Prett/Storey Publishing
Text design and production by Karin Stack
Indexed by Susan Olason, Indexes & Knowledge Maps

Printed in the United States by R.R. Donnelley
10 9 8 7 6 5 4 3 2

Library of Congress Cataloging-in-Publication Data

Chesman, Andrea.
  Mom's best desserts : 100 classic treats that taste as good now as they did then / Andrea Chesman and Fran Raboff.
     p.   cm.
  ISBN 1-58017-480-9
  1. Desserts. 2. Cookery, American. I. Raboff, Fran. II. Title.
  TX773 .C5224 2002
  641.8'6—dc21
                        2002007747

CONTENTS

Introduction

Here is a collection of truly great desserts — chocolate layer cake and blueberry pie, cherry cobbler and apple pandowdy, lemon meringue and chocolate cream pies, strawberry shortcake and grasshopper pie, chocolate chip cookies and gingerbread men, butterscotch pudding and baked apple dumplings. The classics, the originals, the best.

When you want a birthday cake, nothing but mom's tall devil's food cake will do. And when strawberries are finally available locally, your first impulse is to make strawberry shortcake. Likewise, gingerbread brings a smile to a friend laid up with a broken leg, and a creamy rice pudding soothes the soul after a hard week at work. We all have eaten and enjoyed the elaborate restaurant desserts created by trained pastry chefs, but we love the good old, old-fashioned desserts — the ones our moms and grandmoms made — best. That is what this book is about.

One of the heirloom recipes we tested for this book was an old recipe for chocolate cake that came from a Hershey's cocoa tin. At one time or another, probably half the households in the United States ate that cake. The saying may be "as American as apple pie," but the truth of the matter is that apple pie was invented in England. What America can proudly claim as its own is the layer cake, and the chocolate layer cake may be its best example.

Baking powder, the leavening agent in layer cakes, was an American invention. Before the days of baking powder, cakes were leavened with eggs, sometimes with yeast. The egg cakes required a phenomenal amount of beating. Old recipes can be found that begin with "Separate your eggs and beat for five hours . . ." Tall cakes were layers of baked sponge cake, sandwiched with sweetened creams and jellies.

As early as the Middle Ages, professional bakers knew that baked goods could be leavened with alkaline salts. They made something called pearl ash from refined wood ash and from a type of Spanish seaweed. In northern Europe, bakers used refined salts from the ash of deer antlers.

Native Americans added wood ash to their cornmeal cakes to sweeten the batter. (The wood ash also added essential amino acids to the corn, making it a complete protein.) American colonists took the innovation a step further by using sour milk to moisten the corn cakes. When the acid of the sour milk reacted with the alkaline wood ash, bubbles of carbon dioxide were formed, which made the cakes lighter. The colonists called the wood ash *potash,* and later changed the name to *pearl ash.* By the 1790s, America was shipping tons of pearl ash to Europe.

Pearl ash was eventually replaced by saleratus (an early version of baking soda) which was chemically similar. Both require an acid to work — sour milk, buttermilk, chocolate, molasses. Saleratus was sold in little envelopes with recipes printed on the back. Imagine what a vast improvement in the housewife's life saleratus represented! She could make bread without long rising times, cakes without hours of beating eggs.

The ready adoption of saleratus was made possible by the development of the iron cooking range. The cookstove provided the intense heat needed for the chemical activation of saleratus, something that open fireplaces couldn't provide. So the iron cookstove lightened the housewife's load in several ways. Besides freeing her from the slow methods of hearth cookery, it enabled her to utilize time-saving ingredients — such as saleratus and, later, baking soda — in her cooking.

Then it was discovered that baking soda plus cream of tartar could be used in a batter made with fresh milk, rather than sour milk or buttermilk. This signaled the start of the baking powder industry and the American fascination with layer cakes. It also gave rise to the development of countless recipes for quick breads and muffins.

Pies were ever a standard in the American colonies. What better way to use the dried fruits, the moldy apples, the abundance of fresh summer berries than to encase them in a crust made of flour and lard?

From the South come some of our most beloved pies. Sure, apple pie is a favorite — on both sides of the Atlantic — but from the South come pecan pie, chess pie, black bottom pie, and Key lime pie, to name a few. The South was the center of pastry innovations in part because white sugar was plentiful there when the rest of the country still relied on the more heavily flavored molasses and maple syrup. Skillful slave cooks contributed significantly to this period of culinary development. Also, after the Civil War a shortage of dairy cows led to the introduction of canned condensed milk — the creamy base for Key lime pies and countless other chiffon pies. Pie, at any time of the day, even for breakfast, became the rage in the 1800s.

The history of American desserts, indeed American cooking, is a rich one. Following the Native Americans who sweetened corn cakes came the stern Puritans of New England, the industrious Quakers of Pennsylvania, and the prosperous colonists of Virginia. In the far North and again in the South, French colonists also exerted a profound influence. From these beginnings come our deep-dish fruit pies and cobblers, whimsically named fools, and sweet and creamy puddings.

A second wave of immigration brought Scottish–Irish, German, and Dutch cooking. Meanwhile, the African slaves can be credited with bringing both new foods and new techniques to what was to become American cooking. Into this melting pot of international cookery traditions, American foods — cornmeal, maple syrup, and an abundance of fruits and nuts — were stirred.

The very first American cookbook, Eliza Smith's *The Compleat Housewife,* was printed in Williamsburg, Virginia, in 1742 and in New York in 1764. American by imprint only, the book was a best-seller in England. A few more books followed, but until 1796, these cookbooks continued to reflect the culinary arts of England.

We know, however, from diaries and hand-written "receipt" books that a distinctive American cuisine was emerging prior to 1796. New Englanders were eating chowder, Indian pudding, and baked beans sweetened with molasses and maple syrup; Southerners were enjoying beaten biscuits and discovering tomatoes and okra. It wasn't until 1796 that these new foods and dishes were committed to print — in Amelia Simmons's *American Cookery,* which was published in Hartford, Connecticut.

Simmons described herself as an American orphan, suggesting that those who aren't fortunate enough to be privy to the cooking secrets of mother and grandmother must rely on the printed word. And so began, perhaps, the whole tradition of American self-help books.

Mothers and grandmothers would have been a help in those days, even when the aid of a cookbook was available. Recipes in early cookbooks disdained measures and timing. All was approximate, as ingredients and temperatures in fireplaces and cookstove ovens were hardly standardized.

Small wonder, then, that some of our favorite and most enduring desserts are the simplest — layers of fruit and biscuit, fruit in a pastry shell, cookies. Our culinary forebears invented recipes that fit the larder; they had no choice but to bake with what was at hand — flour, sugar, butter, eggs, and fresh and preserved fruit. To make things more interesting, they gave their creations whimsical names, like snickerdoodles, grunts, slumps, buckles, dowdies. Not all names can be explained, but all of these desserts are meant to be enjoyed now, just as much as they were when grandmother and great-grandmother and great-great-grandmother made them.

1 • Cookies

Chocolate Chip Cookies

Does anyone ever outgrow the childhood pleasure of biting into a chewy chocolate chip cookie, still warm from the oven? This is a classic recipe for America's favorite cookie, at its best when served with a glass of cold milk.

2¼ cups sifted unbleached all-purpose flour

1 teaspoon salt

1 cup (2 sticks) butter, at room temperature

¾ cup firmly packed brown sugar

¾ cup granulated sugar

2 large eggs, beaten

1 teaspoon baking soda

1 teaspoon hot water

2 cups (12 ounces) semisweet chocolate chips

1 cup chopped nuts

1 teaspoon pure vanilla extract

1. Preheat the oven to 375°F. Lightly grease two baking sheets.

2. Sift together the flour and salt. Set aside.

3. In a mixing bowl, cream together the butter and brown and granulated sugars. Beat in the eggs. Combine the baking soda and hot water and add to the creamed mixture. Stir in the flour mixture. Then stir in the chocolate chips, nuts, and vanilla.

4. Drop the dough by the teaspoon onto the baking sheets about 1 inch apart.

5. Bake for 8 to 10 minutes, until the cookies are golden.

6. Cool on a wire rack.

About 100 small cookies

birth of the chocolate chip cookie

There was a time, not so long ago, when chocolate came in great slabs; there were no chips, bits, or morsels. In 1933, Mrs. Ruth Wakefield was making a batch of butter dewdrop cookies (or butter dropdos; accounts vary) for the guests at the Toll House Inn, and she was in a rush. Instead of melting the chocolate as her recipe required, she decided to chop up the chocolate and let it melt into the cookies as they baked. The chocolate bits retained their shape, and the chocolate chip cookie was born. At first Mrs. Wakefield called the cookies chocolate crunch cookies (or chocolate crispies, again depending on whose account you read), but soon she changed the name to Toll House cookies. Before long, the recipe was published in a newspaper and sales of Nestlé's chocolate began to rise. Recognizing a good thing when they saw the sales charts, Nestlé's began printing the recipe (with Mrs. Wakefield's permission) on packages of specially scored chocolate bars that broke easily into bits. A few years later, Nestlé's bought the legal rights to use the Toll House trade name and began marketing chocolate chips.

Oatmeal Chocolate Chip Cookies

These cookies are the best of the best: a cross between chocolate chip cookies and oatmeal raisin cookies. It is the combination of cinnamon and chocolate that proves utterly irresistible.

1½ cups unbleached all-purpose flour	¾ cup granulated sugar
1½ teaspoons ground cinnamon	2 large eggs
¾ teaspoon baking powder	2 teaspoons pure vanilla extract
¾ teaspoon baking soda	2 cups rolled oats (not instant)
½ teaspoon salt	1½ cups (9 ounces) chocolate chips
¾ cup (1½ sticks) butter, at room temperature	1 cup chopped walnuts or pecans
¾ cup firmly packed light brown sugar	

1. Preheat the oven to 375°F.

2. In a medium-sized bowl, sift together the flour, cinnamon, baking powder, baking soda, and salt. Set aside.

3. In a large bowl, combine the butter, brown and granulated sugars, eggs, and vanilla. Beat until creamy. Add the flour mixture and beat until blended. Then beat in the oats, chocolate chips, and nuts.

4. Drop rounded tablespoons of the dough 2 inches apart on ungreased baking sheets.

5. Bake for 12 to 15 minutes, until the cookies are golden.

6. Let the cookies cool on the baking sheets for a few minutes. Then use a spatula to carefully transfer the cookies to wire racks to cool completely.

30 to 40 cookies

Oatmeal Cookies

Studded with raisins and nuts, these are satisfying, homey cookies. A bite conjures up images of "Leave-It-to-Beaver" moms and after-school snacks of cookies and milk.

1½ cups unbleached all-purpose flour

1 teaspoon baking soda

1 teaspoon ground cinnamon

½ teaspoon salt

1 cup (2 sticks) butter, at room temperature

1 cup firmly packed dark brown sugar

½ cup granulated sugar

2 large eggs

2 tablespoons molasses

¼ cup hot water

1 teaspoon pure vanilla extract

3 cups rolled oats (not instant)

1½ cups raisins

1 cup chopped walnuts (optional)

1. Preheat the oven to 375°F.

2. Sift together the flour, baking soda, cinnamon, and salt. Set aside.

3. In a large mixing bowl, beat together the butter and brown and granulated sugars until creamy. Add the eggs, one at a time, beating well after each addition. Mix in the molasses, hot water, and vanilla, beating until fluffy. Stir in the flour mixture, blending thoroughly. Add the oats, raisins, and walnuts (if using), stirring until combined.

4. Drop rounded tablespoons of the dough 2 inches apart on ungreased baking sheets. Press with a wet spoon or spatula to flatten.

5. Bake for 12 to 15 minutes, until the cookies are golden.

6. Let the cookies cool on the baking sheets for a few minutes. Then use a spatula to carefully transfer the cookies to wire racks to cool completely.

About 60 cookies

Oh, weary mothers, rolling dough
Don't you wish that food would grow?
How happy all the world would be,
With a cookie bush, and a doughnut tree.

— Mrs. Harold J. Wells
(from *The 20th Century Bride's Cook Book*, 1929)

Peanut Butter Cookies

Peanuts are thought to have originated in Brazil and found their way to Europe with Portuguese explorers. From Europe, peanuts spread throughout the world, making the journey from Africa to North America via African slaves. Since the Civil War, peanuts have been an important agricultural crop in the South, where the little ground nut is also known as a ground-pea and as a goober.

In 1890, peanut butter was invented by a St. Louis doctor who promoted it as a health food. It was an instant hit in the United States. But to most of the world, peanuts are valued primarily as a source of oil and as cattle feed. What a shame!

1¾ cups unbleached all-purpose flour	½ cup firmly packed dark brown sugar
½ teaspoon baking powder	½ cup granulated sugar
½ teaspoon baking soda	1 large egg
½ teaspoon salt	2 tablespoons freshly squeezed orange juice
½ cup (1 stick) butter, at room temperature	1 teaspoon pure vanilla extract
½ cup crunchy peanut butter	½ cup chopped peanuts, to garnish

1. Sift together the flour, baking powder, baking soda, and salt. Set aside.

2. In a large mixing bowl, beat together the butter, peanut butter, and brown and granulated sugars until creamy. Beat in the egg. Mix in the orange juice and vanilla, beating until fluffy. Stir in the flour mixture, blending thoroughly. Wrap and refrigerate the dough for 1 hour, or until firm.

3. Preheat the oven to 350°F.

4. Shape the dough into 1-inch balls. Arrange them 2 inches apart on ungreased baking sheets. Flatten the balls with a wet fork twice, pressing a crisscross pattern into each top. Sprinkle with the chopped peanuts.

5. Bake for 8 to 10 minutes, until the cookies are golden.

6. Let the cookies cool on the baking sheets for a few minutes. Use a spatula to carefully transfer them to wire racks to cool completely.

About 36 cookies

national peanut festival

Some three to four tons of roasted peanuts are consumed at the National Peanut Festival held in Dothan, Alabama, every October — and that's not counting the peanuts that are eaten in the annual bake-off in the form of cookies, pies, ice cream, and candies. That is counting, however, the peanuts that are dumped from cement trucks at the festival parade.

Don't want to miss the festival this year? For dates and more information, contact the National Peanut Festival Association (see Resources, page 198).

Sugar Cookies

George Washington would be surprised to learn that cherry pies are associated with his name. His own favorite dessert was said to be Martha's "sugar cakes," which she rolled thin and cut rather large. These sugar cookies would probably delight old George.

2 cups unbleached all-purpose flour

1 teaspoon baking powder

½ teaspoon salt

1 cup sugar

½ cup (1 stick) butter, at room temperature

1 large egg

1 tablespoon milk

1½ teaspoons pure vanilla extract

Granulated sugar or sugar crystals, to garnish

1. Sift together the flour, baking powder, and salt. Set aside.

2. Beat together the sugar and butter until creamy. Beat in the egg. Mix in the milk and vanilla, beating until fluffy. Stir in the flour mixture, blending thoroughly.

3. Divide the dough in half and wrap each portion in plastic. Refrigerate for 2 hours, or until firm enough to handle.

4. Preheat the oven to 375°F. Lightly grease several baking sheets.

5. Working with one portion of the dough at a time, roll out the dough ⅛ inch thick on a lightly floured work surface. Cut out individual cookies with a 3-inch round cookie cutter. Carefully lift the cookies with a large spatula and transfer to the baking sheets, setting them 1 inch apart. Sprinkle the tops of the cookies with sugar.

6. Bake for 8 to 10 minutes, until the edges are lightly browned.

7. Let the cookies cool on the baking sheets for a few minutes. Then use a spatula to carefully transfer them to wire racks to cool completely.

24 to 30 cookies

rolled cookies

The most difficult part of making rolled cookies is keeping the dough from sticking to the work surface. If too much flour is used, the dough becomes tough. Instead of simply flouring your work surface, try using a mix of equal parts flour and confectioners' sugar.

Scottish Shortbread

There's no question about the origin of these buttery morsels. There was a significant wave of Scottish immigration to the South in the early 1700s, and with the immigrants came shortbread (*short,* or shortening, in the form of butter, and *bread* because these cookies aren't particularly sweet). This recipe makes very buttery, very crisp shortbreads, as close to the traditional old-time Scottish shortbread flavor as possible.

1½ cups sifted unbleached all-purpose flour	¼ teaspoon salt
1 cup sifted confectioners' sugar	1 cup (2 sticks) butter, cut into small pieces
½ cup cornstarch	1 teaspoon pure vanilla extract

1. Preheat the oven to 325°F.

2. In a large mixing bowl, combine the flour, sugar, cornstarch, and salt.

3. Using your fingers, blend the butter and vanilla into the flour mixture until fully absorbed. Shape the dough into a pancake, then knead or mix well for 10 minutes. (With an electric mixer, beat for 5 minutes.)

4. Transfer the dough to an ungreased 8- or 9-inch square baking pan, a 9-inch round pie plate, or a 9-inch pan with a removable bottom. Flatten the dough into an even layer. If the dough is too sticky to spread, refrigerate it for a few minutes first. With a knife, score the dough partway through and mark into squares or wedges. Prick the surface of the shortbread with a fork.

5. Bake for 30 minutes, or until the shortbread is light golden. Do not overbake.

6. Cut into squares or wedges while still hot. Cool on a rack before removing from the pan.

36 squares or 12 wedges

Snickerdoodles

Like many American cookies, these are probably the invention of the Pennsylvania Dutch. We're not sure what the name conjures up (it's probably a nonsense word), but snickerdoodles emerge from the oven as round little pillows delicately flavored with a cinnamon-and-sugar coating.

2¾ cups unbleached all-purpose flour
1 teaspoon baking soda
1 teaspoon cream of tartar
½ teaspoon salt
¼ teaspoon freshly grated nutmeg

1⅓ cups plus 3 tablespoons sugar
1 cup butter or vegetable shortening, at room temperature
2 large eggs
1 teaspoon pure vanilla extract
1 tablespoon ground cinnamon

1. Sift together the flour, baking soda, cream of tartar, salt, and nutmeg. Set aside.

2. In a large mixing bowl, beat together 1⅓ cups of the sugar and the butter until creamy. Add the eggs, one at a time, beating well after each addition. Add the vanilla. Stir in the flour mixture, blending thoroughly.

3. Wrap and refrigerate the dough for 1 hour.

4. Preheat the oven to 375°F.

5. Combine the cinnamon and the remaining 3 tablespoons of sugar in a small bowl. Shape the dough into 1-inch balls. Roll the balls in the cinnamon-sugar. Arrange the cookies 2 inches apart on ungreased baking sheets.

6. Bake for 12 minutes, or until the cookies are golden.

7. Transfer the cookies to wire racks to cool completely.

About 60 cookies

baking cookies

Unless a recipe specifies otherwise, cookies can be baked two cookie sheets at a time. If the baking sheets don't fit on the oven rack side by side, place them on the middle and bottom racks. Halfway through the baking time, switch the trays and rotate them 180 degrees for even baking.

Cinnamon-Sugar Icebox Cookies

Iceboxes were invented in 1802 by Maryland farmer Thomas Moore, who designed an insulated "ice box" for keeping food cold. By the 1830s, these iceboxes were found in most kitchens, giving rise to the "ice man" who cometh with 100-pound blocks of ice that were harvested from frozen northern lakes. It wasn't too long before enterprising bakers discovered they could keep logs of cookie dough in the icebox, ready to be baked whenever fresh-baked cookies were desired.

3 cups unbleached all-purpose flour	1 cup plus 2 tablespoons granulated sugar
1 teaspoon baking powder	¼ cup firmly packed light brown sugar
½ teaspoon baking soda	½ cup sour cream, at room temperature
½ teaspoon salt	1 tablespoon pure vanilla extract
1 cup (2 sticks) butter, at room temperature	½ teaspoon ground cinnamon

1. Sift together the flour, baking powder, baking soda, and salt. Set aside.

2. In a large bowl, beat the butter with 1 cup of the granulated sugar and the brown sugar until creamy. Mix in the sour cream and vanilla. Stir in the flour mixture, blending thoroughly.

3. Divide the dough into four parts. Using a doubled sheet of waxed paper as a guide, roll each part into a tight smooth log about 6 inches long and 2 inches in diameter. Wrap in waxed paper and aluminum foil. Freeze until firm, about 2 hours. (They slice best when frozen.)

4. Preheat the oven to 350°F. Lightly grease several baking sheets. Combine the remaining 2 tablespoons of granulated sugar with the cinnamon.

5. With a very sharp thin knife, thinly slice the cookies (about ³⁄₁₆-inch thick). Place the cookies 1 inch apart on the prepared baking sheets. Sprinkle lightly with the cinnamon-sugar.

6. Bake for 10 to 12 minutes, until lightly golden around the edges.

7. Use a spatula to carefully transfer the cookies to wire racks to cool completely.

About 120 small cookies

Mocha-Glazed Chocolate Icebox Cookies

A chocolate cookie for grown-ups. Try a few of these not-too-sweet cookies with coffee; but they are even better with vanilla ice cream.

Cookies

1¼ cups unbleached all-purpose flour

1 teaspoon baking powder

1 teaspoon instant coffee powder

¼ teaspoon salt

¾ cup sugar

½ cup (1 stick) butter, at room temperature

3 ounces unsweetened chocolate, melted

1 large egg

1 teaspoon vanilla extract

Mocha Glaze

1 cup confectioners' sugar

3 tablespoons unsweetened cocoa powder

2 tablespoons hot brewed coffee (plus 1 teaspoon, if needed)

1 tablespoon butter

½ teaspoon pure vanilla extract

1. Sift together the flour, baking powder, coffee, and salt. Set aside.

2. In a large bowl, beat the sugar and butter until creamy. Stir in the chocolate. Add the egg and vanilla and beat until well combined. Stir in the flour mixture, blending thoroughly.

3. Divide the dough into two parts. Using a doubled sheet of waxed paper as a guide, roll each part into a tight smooth log about 6 inches long and 2 inches in diameter. Wrap in waxed paper and aluminum foil. Refrigerate until firm, about 2 hours. (They slice best when refrigerated, not frozen.)

4. While the dough chills, prepare the glaze. Into a small bowl, sift together the confectioners' sugar and cocoa. Mix together the hot coffee, butter, and vanilla. Gradually add to the confectioners' sugar mixture and stir until smooth. If the glaze is too thick to spread, stir in another teaspoon of coffee. Cover and set aside.

5. Preheat the oven to 350°F. Lightly grease several baking sheets.

6. With a very sharp thin knife, thinly slice the cookies (about ³⁄₁₆-inch thick). Place the cookies 1 inch apart on the prepared baking sheets.

7. Bake for 8 to 10 minutes, until the cookies are almost firm to the touch and just beginning to get slightly darker around the edges. Watch carefully because they burn easily.

8. Use a spatula to carefully transfer the cookies to wire racks. While the cookies are still warm, brush with the glaze. Cool until set.

About 60 small cookies

overbrowned cookies

The most common reason why cookies burn is that the baker was distracted. The very best way to avoid overbaking cookies is to set a timer each time a batch goes in.

If you are baking on dark baking sheets, your cookies may overbrown. Lining dark sheets with aluminum foil will help to avoid this problem. Insulated cookie sheets (two sheets of aluminum with an air pocket between them) are another solution. You may have to allow an extra minute or two for baking.

Brandy Snaps

Brandy snaps are cookies flavored with brandy, ginger, and molasses, close cousins to gingersnaps. They date at least as far back as the Middle Ages, when they were popular items at fairs in England. In particular, brandy snaps are associated with the Nottingham Fair, which was held annually on the first Thursday in October and was famous as the premier showcase for geese. People came from all over the English Midlands to select their geese, which were driven there in flocks by gooseherds armed only with crooks to keep the cantankerous geese in line.

1 cup unbleached all-purpose flour

½ cup sugar

½ teaspoon ground ginger

⅛ teaspoon salt

½ cup light molasses

½ cup (1 stick) butter

2 tablespoons brandy

1. Preheat the oven to 325°F.

2. Mix together the flour, sugar, ginger, and salt. Set aside.

3. In a medium-sized saucepan, heat the molasses just to the boiling point. Stir in the butter. Add the flour mixture gradually and cook, stirring, until hot and blended. Remove from the heat. Add the brandy.

4. Place the pan over hot water to keep the mixture soft. Drop by the teaspoon 3 inches apart onto ungreased baking sheets. Allow about six cookies to each sheet because the cookies will spread as they bake.

5. Bake for 7 to 8 minutes, until bubbly and golden.

6. Cool the cookies on the baking sheets for about 2 minutes, until the cookies hold together. Using a wide spatula, quickly loosen one cookie at a time and place it on a paper towel or drape it over a rolling pin to cool in a curved shape. If the cookies harden before they are removed from the baking sheets, reheat in the oven for 1 minute.

7. When the cookies are cool, store immediately in an airtight container.

NOTE: You can shape brandy snaps into a cylinder by forming them around a wooden spoon or dowel; the ends then can be dipped into melted chocolate. Large brandy snaps can be filled with whipped cream or ice cream, piped in with a pastry bag. Serve ice cream–filled brandy snaps with chocolate sauce or hot fudge.

About 36 cookies

cookie slang

In the Wild West, a cookie was the cook or the cook's helper, not a delectable dessert. The name was one of the more benign slang terms that were used. Wouldn't you rather be called "cookie" than "bean master," "belly cheater," "biscuit roller," "dough puncher," "grease burner," "grub spoiler," "gut burglar," "hash slinger," "mess moll," "pot rustler," or "sizzler"? A waitress in a restaurant was known as a "cookie pusher."

Sand Tarts

So rich and buttery, these cookies crumble like sand as you bite into them.

2 cups unbleached all-purpose flour

1 teaspoon baking powder

¼ teaspoon salt

1 cup plus 2 tablespoons sugar

½ cup (1 stick) butter, at room temperature

2 large eggs

1 teaspoon finely grated orange zest

1 teaspoon orange or vanilla extract

2 teaspoons water

½ teaspoon ground cinnamon

½ cup slivered almonds, to garnish

1. Sift together the flour, baking powder, and salt. Set aside.

2. In a large mixing bowl, beat together 1 cup of the sugar and the butter until creamy. Separate one of the eggs. Beat in one whole egg and one egg yolk and add to the butter mixture. Reserve the remaining white. Add the orange zest and orange extract to the mixture and beat until fluffy. Stir in the flour mixture, blending thoroughly.

3. Divide the dough in two parts and wrap each in plastic. Refrigerate for 2 hours, or until firm.

4. Preheat the oven to 350°F.

5. Working with one portion of the dough at a time, roll out the dough ⅛-inch thick on a lightly floured work surface. Cut the dough into squares or diamonds. Carefully lift the cookies with a spatula and transfer to ungreased baking sheets, setting them about 2 inches apart.

6. Make an egg wash by combining the remaining egg white with the water. Brush the tops of the cookies with the egg wash. Combine the remaining 2 tablespoons of sugar with the cinnamon and sprinkle on top of the cookies. Garnish with the slivered almonds.

7. Bake the cookies for 8 to 10 minutes, until the edges turn golden.

8. Let the cookies cool on the baking sheets for a few minutes. Then use a spatula to carefully transfer them to wire racks to cool completely.

36 to 48 cookies

Pecan Tassies

Tarts, tartlets, tassies. Tassies are the tiniest of tarts, a finger tart that disappears in just two bites. Pecan tassies are miniature pecan pies.

Cookie Shells

- ½ cup (1 stick) butter, at room temperature
- 1 small package (3 ounces) cream cheese, at room temperature
- 1 cup unbleached all-purpose flour
- ⅛ teaspoon salt

Filling

- 1 large egg
- ¾ cup firmly packed dark brown sugar
- 1 tablespoon butter, at room temperature
- 1 teaspoon pure vanilla extract
- ⅛ teaspoon salt
- ¾ cup chopped pecans
- Confectioners' sugar

1. To make the cookie shells, combine the butter and cream cheese and beat until well blended. Stir in the flour and salt, mixing until well combined. Gather together the dough in a ball, wrap in plastic film, and chill for at least 1 hour.

2. Divide the dough into 24 pieces and roll each piece into a ball about 1 inch in diameter. Press each ball into the bottom and sides of 24 mini-muffin cups.

3. Preheat the oven to 325°F.

4. To make the filling, beat together the egg, brown sugar, butter, vanilla, and salt. Stir in the pecans. Spoon the filling into the cookie shells.

5. Bake for 20 to 25 minutes, until the cookie shells are golden and firm to the touch. The tops of the filling will be crackled.

6. Cool on wire racks for 20 to 25 minutes. To remove the pecan tassies from the pan, insert a small knife around the edge of each cookie shell to loosen it, then slip it out. When cool, sprinkle with the confectioners' sugar.

24 cookies

Molasses Cookies

Molasses wasn't exactly the sweetener of choice in early American cooking; it was just about the only affordable sweetener (honey and maple syrup were available in limited quantities, depending on where you lived). In the early days of the republic, molasses played an important role in making slave trading lucrative. Slavers would capture Africans to fill their ships bound for the West Indies. In the West Indies, the slaves would be sold and the empty ships loaded with barrels of molasses bound for the States, where much of the molasses was distilled into rum. Then the ships would carry timber and other New World products back to Europe. Abolitionists in New England called for a boycott of molasses and exhorted people to use maple syrup instead. "Make your own sugar," was the advice of the *Farmer's Almanac* in 1803, "and send not to the Indies for it. Feast not on the toil, pain, and misery of the wretched."

Eventually, growing cane sugar and sugar beet industries made white sugar affordable, and this sugar replaced molasses in most recipes.

2¼ cups unbleached all-purpose flour	¼ teaspoon salt
2 teaspoons baking soda	1 cup firmly packed dark brown sugar
1 teaspoon ground cinnamon	¾ cup (1½ sticks) butter, at room temperature
½ teaspoon ground ginger	1 large egg
¼ teaspoon ground allspice	⅓ cup dark molasses
¼ teaspoon ground cloves	Granulated sugar

1. Preheat the oven to 375°F. Lightly grease two baking sheets.

2. Sift together the flour, baking soda, cinnamon, ginger, allspice, cloves, and salt. Set aside.

3. In a large mixing bowl, beat together the brown sugar and butter until creamy. Beat in the egg and molasses. Stir in the flour mixture, blending thoroughly. (If the dough is too soft to handle, chill in the refrigerator for 1 hour.)

4. Shape the cookie dough into balls the size of walnuts. Dip the top of each ball into white sugar. Place them, sugar-side up, 2 inches apart, on the prepared baking sheets.

5. Bake for 10 to 12 minutes, until lightly browned.

6. Transfer the cookies to wire racks to cool.

About 48 cookies

joe froggers

In another time and place, molasses cookies were also called Joe Froggers. It seems that in Marblehead, Massachusetts, there lived an old African-American gentleman who was known as Uncle Joe. Uncle Joe lived on the edge of a frog pond and enjoyed a certain reputation for making the best cookies in town, as large as lily pads and as dark as the frogs in the pond. Seamen stocked up on Joe Froggers, as they kept well in sea chests, and spread the fame of these cookies when they traded them for rum.

Gingery Gingersnaps

Gingersnaps probably have their origin with the Pennsylvania Dutch, and their name probably comes from the word *snappen,* which means "easy." The cookies are rolled in sugar before baking, giving them a lovely, crinkly top.

1⅓ cups unbleached all-purpose flour

½ teaspoon baking soda

⅛ teaspoon salt

2 tablespoons dark molasses

1 tablespoon warm brewed coffee

6 tablespoons butter, at room temperature

¼ cup plus 3 tablespoons granulated sugar

¼ cup firmly packed brown sugar

1 teaspoon ground ginger

½ teaspoon ground cinnamon

¼ teaspoon ground cloves

½ cup finely chopped crystallized ginger

1. Sift together the flour, baking soda, and salt. Set aside.

2. In a small bowl, combine the molasses and coffee.

3. In a mixing bowl, cream together the butter, ¼ cup of the granulated sugar, the brown sugar, ginger, cinnamon, and cloves. Add the molasses mixture and flour mixture, beating until well blended. Stir in the crystallized ginger. Gather together the dough in a ball, wrap in plastic wrap, and chill for at least 1 hour, or until firm.

4. Preheat the oven to 350°F. Lightly grease two baking sheets.

5. Shape the dough into 1-inch balls. Roll the balls in 2 tablespoons of the granulated sugar. Place them on the baking sheets about 2 inches apart. Press down each cookie with the bottom of a glass dipped in the remaining 1 tablespoon of granulated sugar until cookies are nice and thin.

6. Bake, one sheet at a time, for about 10 minutes. Remove the cookies from the oven before the edges of the cookies start to brown; they will be soft in the center but will harden when cool. Watch the cookies carefully and do not allow them to scorch.

7. Transfer the cookies to wire racks to cool.

About 40 cookies

Gingerbread Men

Traditionally eaten at Christmastime, these cookies are welcome any time of the year. Legend has it that Queen Elizabeth I of England invented gingerbread men.

2½ cups unbleached all-purpose flour

2 teaspoons ground ginger

½ teaspoon baking soda

½ teaspoon ground cinnamon

¼ teaspoon ground allspice

¼ teaspoon salt

4 tablespoons butter, at room temperature

¼ cup solid vegetable shortening, at room temperature

½ cup firmly packed light brown sugar

½ cup dark molasses

2 tablespoons water

Currants or raisins and cinnamon candies

1. Sift together the flour, ginger, baking soda, cinnamon, allspice, and salt. Set aside.

2. In a large mixing bowl, combine the butter and shortening. Beat until creamy. Add the brown sugar gradually and beat until fluffy. Stir in the molasses and water. Add the flour mixture, mixing until well blended.

3. Wrap the dough in plastic wrap and refrigerate until chilled, 1 to 2 hours.

4. Preheat the oven to 375°F. Lightly grease two baking sheets.

5. On a lightly floured work surface, roll out the dough to a thickness of about ³⁄₁₆ inch. Cut with gingerbread cookie cutters. Carefully lift the cookies with a large spatula and transfer them to the baking sheets. Decorate with currants or raisins and cinnamon candies.

6. Bake for 8 to 10 minutes, until set.

7. Let the cookies cool on the baking sheets for a few minutes. Then use a spatula to carefully transfer them to wire racks to cool completely.

12 to 16 cookies

Hermits

Looking for a spice cookie with good keeping qualities? Look no further. These are great cookies to make when you have the time to do a little baking in advance of the potluck or bake sale. Hermits will keep in an airtight container for at least a week.

1⅓ cups unbleached all-purpose flour

1 teaspoon ground cinnamon

½ teaspoon baking soda

½ teaspoon grated nutmeg

¼ teaspoon ground allspice

¼ teaspoon ground cloves

¼ teaspoon salt

1 cup firmly packed dark brown sugar

½ cup (1 stick) butter, at room temperature

1 large egg

½ cup sour cream

1 teaspoon pure vanilla extract

1 cup chopped raisins or dried currants

¾ cup chopped walnuts or hickory nuts

1. Preheat the oven to 350°F. Lightly grease several baking sheets.

2. Sift together the flour, cinnamon, baking soda, nutmeg, allspice, cloves, and salt. Set aside.

3. In a large mixing bowl, beat together the sugar and butter until creamy. Add the egg and beat until fluffy. Mix in the sour cream and vanilla. Stir in the flour mixture, blending thoroughly. Add the raisins and nuts, stirring until combined.

4. Arrange rounded teaspoons of the cookie dough 2 inches apart on the baking sheets.

5. Bake for 12 to 15 minutes, until the cookies are golden.

6. Transfer the cookies to wire racks to cool completely.

About 48 cookies

hermit history

The older the recipe, the more likely it is that there will be some fanciful stories behind its origins. In the case of the hermit, we know that the first printed reference dates back to only 1896, but the cookie seems to be much older. Sometimes hermits were called "Harwich hermits," suggesting that they originated in Harwich, Massachusetts. It is thought that seamen took these cookies with them on trading ships because the dried fruits kept the cookies soft and fresh-tasting for a while. Some writers have speculated that the name refers to the cookies' long keeping nature — they're best when hidden away like a hermit for several days. Others say that the name refers to their brown lumpy appearance, which resembles a hermit's robe.

There is no dispute about what makes a hermit. It is a spicy, chewy cookie studded with raisins or currants. But bar cookie or drop cookie? That is the question. Miss Fanny Farmer made her hermits as drop cookies in the 1896 edition of her famous cookbook. Round or square, they are delicious cookies, great to pack in sea chests or lunch boxes.

Spritz Cookies

These pretty little cookies came to the United States with Scandinavian immigrants, who brought their cookie presses with them. The name comes from the German word *spritzen,* which means "to squirt or spray."

2¼ cups unbleached all-purpose flour

¼ cup cornstarch

½ teaspoon baking powder

¼ teaspoon salt

1 cup (2 sticks) butter, at room temperature

¾ cup sugar

1 large egg or 2 large egg yolks

1 teaspoon pure vanilla extract

½ teaspoon almond extract

Colored sugar crystals, chocolate sprinkles, finely chopped nuts, or halved candied cherries, to garnish

1. Preheat the oven to 375°F.

2. Sift together the flour, cornstarch, baking powder, and salt. Set aside.

3. In a large mixing bowl, beat together the butter and sugar until creamy. Beat in the egg. Mix in the vanilla and almond extracts, beating until fluffy. Stir in the flour mixture, mixing well.

4. Pack the dough into a cookie press fitted with a decorative plate. Press the dough onto ungreased baking sheets, 1 inch apart. Decorate with the assorted garnishes.

5. Bake for 10 minutes, or until the edges of the cookies are lightly browned.

6. Transfer the cookies to wire racks to cool completely.

NOTE: If you don't have a cookie press, you can still make these cookies. Shape the dough into 1-inch balls. Flatten each ball with a glass that has been dipped in granulated sugar or make a crisscross design on the cookies by pressing down with a fork. Or roll the dough into ¼-inch ropes and form into pretzel shapes. Bake as instructed above.

VARIATIONS

Chocolate Spritz: Add 2 ounces of melted bittersweet chocolate or semisweet chocolate to the butter and sugar.

Spice Spritz: Add ½ teaspoon ground cinnamon, ¼ teaspoon ground cloves, and ¼ teaspoon freshly grated nutmeg to the flour mixture.

48 to 60 cookies

A s soon as school is out at night
All children, near and far,
Go rushing home, in one mad flight,
To find the Cooky jar!
(So keep it filled for their delight;
You know how children are.)

— Anon.

Whoopie Pies

Whoops of joy may have inspired the name of these cookie sandwiches, which are probably Pennsylvania Dutch in origin. Add chocolate frosting and you have a Moon Pie, which is the trademarked name for a cookie made by the Chattanooga Bakery in Chattanooga, Tennessee. Moon Pies have been made since 1917 and have proved to be so popular that the company now produces 300,000 Moon Pies a day. This recipe yields considerably fewer.

Cookies

2 cups unbleached all-purpose flour
½ cup unsweetened cocoa powder
1 teaspoon baking soda
½ teaspoon salt
1 cup sugar
½ cup vegetable shortening
1 large egg
1 teaspoon pure vanilla extract
½ cup buttermilk or plain yogurt
½ cup hot coffee

Filling

¾ cup vegetable shortening or butter, at room temperature
1½ cups confectioners' sugar, or more as needed
6 tablespoons Marshmallow Fluff
1 egg white
1 teaspoon pure vanilla extract
Pinch of salt

1. Preheat the oven to 350°F. Grease several baking sheets.

2. In a medium-sized bowl, sift together the flour, cocoa, baking soda, and salt. Set aside.

3. In a large mixing bowl, combine the sugar and shortening. Beat until light and fluffy. Add the egg and vanilla and beat until thoroughly blended. Add one third of the flour mixture alternately with one third of the buttermilk and coffee and beat until smooth. Repeat, adding the flour mixture and liquids in thirds and beating until smooth. The batter will be thicker than cake batter, thinner than cookie dough.

4. Using a small (1½-ounce) ice-cream scoop, drop the batter onto the baking sheets about 2 inches apart.

5. Bake the cookies for about 8 minutes, until the tops appear dry and cracked. Do not overbake.

6. Transfer the cookies onto a wire rack to cool.

7. To make the filling, in a large mixing bowl combine the shortening with the confectioners' sugar, Marshmallow Fluff, egg white, vanilla, and salt. Beat until light and smooth. If the filling seems loose (it will be if you have used butter), add a little more confectioners' sugar to stiffen.

8. Spread half the cookie bottoms with the filling and sandwich each with another cookie.

9. Serve immediately or cover well and store the whoopie pies in the refrigerator until you are ready to serve them. Bring to room temperature before serving.

NOTES:

• The egg white in this recipe is not cooked. Please see "Egg Information" on page 198.

• The filling can be made with vegetable shortening (such as Crisco) or with butter, depending on the desired result. Using vegetable shortening results in a whoopie pie that tastes just like the kind you may remember from a bakery. It has a nice, smooth mouth feel. Butter in the filling tastes richer, more homemade, and is slightly greasy. We prefer the taste and feel of Crisco, but the idea of butter.

• Using an ice-cream scoop to portion out the dough guarantees that each cookie is roughly the same size and shape, making sandwiching them easier. If you don't have a small ice-cream scoop, use generously rounded tablespoons.

14 cookies

Chocolate Coconut Macaroons

Sometimes called Coconut Drop Kisses, these cookies are often featured on Jewish tables for the Passover holiday, during which no wheat, other than matzohs, is served. They make a delicious cookie any time of the year.

1 can (14 ounces) sweetened condensed milk

1 teaspoon pure vanilla extract

1/3 cup unsweetened cocoa powder

1/4 teaspoon salt

3 cups lightly packed, sweetened flaked coconut

1. Preheat the oven to 325°F. Line several baking sheets with parchment paper or aluminum foil. Grease well.

2. In a large bowl, combine the condensed milk, vanilla, cocoa, and salt, mixing until blended. Add the coconut and stir until well combined. Drop by large teaspoonfuls onto the baking sheets, placing them about 2 inches apart.

3. Bake, one sheet at a time, for about 10 minutes, or until the cookies are firm. Watch carefully because the bottoms will burn quickly.

4. Transfer the cookies to wire racks to cool completely.

About 40 cookies

Chocolate Meringue Kisses

Old cookbooks might call these "forgotten cookies" because they were baked last as the oven cooled after a session of baking breads or cakes. The baker would put the kisses in the "slack oven" and avoid looking into the oven as they slowly baked, lest more heat was lost. Under those circumstances, the kisses were sometimes forgotten.

3 large egg whites, at room temperature

⅛ teaspoon cream of tartar

⅛ teaspoon salt

1 cup sugar

3 tablespoons unsweetened cocoa powder

1 cup semisweet chocolate chips

½ cup chopped hazelnuts or walnuts

½ teaspoon pure vanilla extract

1. Preheat the oven to 250°F. Line two baking sheets with aluminum foil. Lightly grease the foil, then sprinkle with flour to coat. Shake out any excess flour.

2. In the large bowl of an electric mixer, beat the egg whites until foamy. Add the cream of tartar and salt and beat until soft peaks form. Gradually sprinkle in the sugar, 1 tablespoon at a time, beating well after each addition. Continue beating until the egg whites are stiff but not dry. The egg whites should hold their shape and remain moist. Sift the cocoa over the mixture. With a rubber spatula, fold the cocoa into the mixture along with the chocolate chips, nuts, and vanilla.

3. Drop the batter by the teaspoonful onto the prepared baking sheets, bringing up the spoon through the meringue to shape like Hershey's Kisses.

4. Bake for 25 to 30 minutes, until crisp.

5. Let the cookies cool on the baking sheets for a few minutes. Then use a spatula to carefully transfer them to wire racks to cool completely. These cookies are best when freshly made, but they will keep for 3 to 4 days in an airtight container.

NOTE: To remove hazelnut skins, toast the nuts in a 300°F oven for 12 to 15 minutes, stirring occasionally. Place the nuts in a cloth towel and rub to remove the skins.

48 cookies

Chocolate Brownies

One often reads about the importance of the Sears, Roebuck catalog to rural America in the nineteenth century, but who would have guessed that the first published chocolate brownie recipe appeared in that catalog in 1897?

2 ounces semisweet chocolate, or ⅓ cup semisweet chocolate chips

2 ounces unsweetened chocolate

½ cup (1 stick) butter

1 cup sugar

¼ teaspoon salt

1 teaspoon pure vanilla extract

2 large eggs

½ cup unbleached all-purpose flour

½ cup chopped walnuts

1. Preheat the oven to 350°F. Lightly grease and flour an 8-inch square baking pan.

2. In a medium-sized, heavy-bottomed saucepan, melt the chocolates and butter over low heat, stirring until smooth. Remove from the heat and stir in the sugar and salt. Add the vanilla and eggs, one at a time, beating well after each addition. Stir in the flour and nuts, mixing until blended. Spoon the batter into the prepared pan.

3. Bake for about 25 minutes, or until the top feels dry and looks shiny. The inside will be soft, but will firm up when cooled.

4. Cool the brownies completely in the pan on a rack, then cut into squares.

16 to 22 bars

chocolate chat

Ever since a certain Dr. James Baker invested in the first chocolate mill in the New World, Americans have conducted a love affair with chocolate, and they buy Baker brand chocolate to this day for their cakes, brownies, and cookies.

Recently, though, Americans have begun to take note of other high-quality brands, imported and domestic. To determine whether a chocolate is of high quality, look for cocoa butter in the ingredients list. Only the good brands have it; others use less-expensive vegetable oils, which extend the shelf life of the chocolate by maintaining its fresh appearance, but they don't do much for the flavor.

Chocolate quality is actually determined during the manufacturing process. After they are picked, cocoa beans are fermented; then they are processed to separate the cocoa butter from the rest of the bean. What is left is called chocolate liquor. During the manufacture of high-quality chocolate, the cocoa butter (or vegetable oil) is remixed with the chocolate liquor. Sugar may be added to make semisweet, bitter-sweet, or sweet chocolate; milk solids may be added for milk chocolate.

Lecithin may be added along with the cocoa butter to improve the viscosity. It also allows more of the chocolate flavor, which can be masked by pure cocoa butter, to come through.

You can substitute unsweetened cocoa powder for unsweetened chocolate, using 3 tablespoons of cocoa plus 1 tablespoon of vegetable oil for every ounce of chocolate.

Lemon Bars

This recipe makes a rich, buttery cookie. It is a good idea to place the cut bars on paper towels to absorb some of the excess butter. For variation, consider sprinkling the bars with coconut flakes instead of the powdered sugar.

Cookie Crust

2 cups unbleached all-purpose flour

½ cup plus 2 to 3 tablespoons confectioners' sugar

Pinch of salt

1 teaspoon finely grated lemon zest

1 cup (2 sticks) butter, at room temperature

Lemon Filling

4 large eggs

2 cups granulated sugar

1 tablespoon finely grated lemon zest

6 tablespoons freshly squeezed lemon juice

2 tablespoons unbleached all-purpose flour

1 teaspoon baking powder

1. Preheat the oven to 350°F. Lightly grease a 9- by 13-inch baking pan.

2. To make the cookie crust, combine the flour, confectioners' sugar, and salt. Add the lemon zest and butter, mixing until thoroughly blended. Using the heel of your hand or the back of a spoon, gently spread the mixture over the bottom of the pan. Bake for 20 minutes.

3. While the crust is baking, prepare the filling. Beat the eggs until light. Gradually add the sugar, beating until thick and lemon colored. Add the lemon zest, lemon juice, flour, and baking powder, blending until well combined.

4. Pour the lemon mixture over the still-warm baked cookie crust.

5. Bake for 20 to 25 minutes, until the top is a golden brown. The filling should be soft.

6. To garnish, sift the remaining 2 to 3 tablespoons confectioners' sugar over the cookies while they are still warm. Cool on a rack for at least 30 minutes before cutting into squares or bars.

About 35 bars

Raspberry Bars

Raspberries are our favorite, but any berry can be used to make these bars.

Bottom Layer

2 cups unbleached all-purpose flour

¾ cup confectioners' sugar

½ cup (1 stick) butter, melted

½ teaspoon pure vanilla extract

Top Layer

2 cups rolled oats (or 1 cup rolled oats and 1 cup quick oats)

1 cup firmly packed light brown sugar

½ cup (1 stick) butter, melted

1 teaspoon ground cinnamon

Filling

2 cups fresh or frozen raspberries, thawed

½ cup granulated sugar

2 tablespoons quick-cooking tapioca

1. Preheat the oven to 325°F. Lightly butter a 9- by 13-inch baking pan.

2. To make the bottom layer, combine the flour, confectioners' sugar, butter, and vanilla. Mix with a fork until the butter is evenly distributed and the mixture is crumbly. Firmly pat the mixture into the bottom of the baking dish. Bake for 15 minutes. Set aside to cool.

3. While the bottom layer bakes, make the filling. Combine the raspberries, granulated sugar, and tapioca. Set aside for at least 30 minutes to allow the tapioca to blend with the raspberry juice.

4. To make the top layer, mix the oats, brown sugar, butter, and cinnamon in a medium-sized bowl and stir until crumbly.

5. When the bottom layer has cooled, spread the filling evenly over it. Sprinkle the oat mixture (top layer) over the raspberries. Bake for 25 to 30 minutes, until the top is golden.

6. Cool completely on a wire rack. Cut into squares or rectangles.

15 to 18 bars

Blondies

Difficult though it is to imagine, there are people who don't care for chocolate. Even more painful to contemplate is the thought that some people are allergic to chocolate. For these people, the blondie was invented: a chocolate-free brownie.

4 tablespoons butter

1 cup firmly packed brown sugar

⅛ teaspoon salt

1 large egg

1 teaspoon pure vanilla extract

½ cup sifted unbleached all-purpose flour

¼ teaspoon baking soda

1 cup coarsely chopped walnuts, lightly toasted

1. Preheat the oven to 350°F. Lightly grease and flour an 8-inch square baking pan.

2. In a medium-sized saucepan, melt the butter over low heat. Remove from the heat and stir in the sugar and salt. Beat in the egg and vanilla. Stir in the flour and baking soda, mixing until blended. Mix in the nuts. Spoon into the prepared pan.

3. Bake for 18 to 20 minutes, or until the blondie begins to pull away from the sides of the pan and is still slightly soft in the middle. Do not overbake.

4. Cool completely in the pan on a wire rack. Cut into squares or rectangles.

NOTE: To toast the walnuts, place in a shallow baking pan and toast in the preheated 350°F oven for 8 to 10 minutes, until fragrant.

16 to 22 bars

the secret of bar cookies

Bar cookies and brownies should come out of the pan with precise, square corners and neat straight edges. What's the secret to success? Let them cool completely in the pan, preferably overnight. If you are baking for your family, then by all means make up a batch of brownies and serve them warm, right out of the oven. Nothing tastes better. But if you are making brownies, blondies, or bar cookies for a dessert buffet or bake sale, it is best to make them the day before. Then when you cut them, the edges will be straight and the neat appearance will be accomplished.

Another way to guarantee straight edges is to bake the bar cookies in a pan lined with aluminum foil. Cut the foil long enough to overhang the edges of the pan. Grease the foil if the recipe calls for a greased pan. Once the cookies are baked and cooled, use the overhanging foil to lift the entire batch of cookies out of the pan. Then cut the cookies with a long knife — you can even use a straightedge to guarantee equal-size pieces. The foil will also save on cleanup and prevent knife marks in the pan.

Dream Bars

Why are these tooth-achingly sweet bar cookies called dream bars? Perhaps because they are the perfect answer to the recurrent waking nightmare every parent experiences. It happens just as you are tucking the little darlings into bed and one of them says, "Oh, I forgot to tell you, but I have to bring in something for the school bake sale tomorrow." These cookies are also known as seven-layer bars and lazy layer bars, for obvious reasons: All you have do is layer up the ingredients, no mixing, no fussing. They are also known as congo bars — an odd name for an all-American favorite.

½ cup (1 stick) butter, melted

1¼ cups graham cracker crumbs

1 cup (6 ounces) semisweet chocolate chips

1 cup (6 ounces) butterscotch morsels

1 cup (about 3 ounces) lightly packed, sweetened flaked coconut

1 can (14 ounces) sweetened condensed milk

1 cup chopped pecans

1. Preheat the oven to 350°F. Spread the butter in a 9- by 13-inch baking dish.

2. Sprinkle the graham cracker crumbs evenly over the butter. Pat to make a firm, level surface with the crumbs. Sprinkle the chocolate chips over the crumbs. Sprinkle the butterscotch morsels over the chocolate. Then sprinkle the coconut over the butterscotch. Drizzle the condensed milk evenly over the entire pan. Finally, sprinkle the pecans over all.

3. Bake for about 20 minutes, until the bars are golden.

4. Cool completely, then cut into bars. These bars improve in flavor after 1 day.

NOTES:

• If you are using a glass baking dish, you can melt the butter in the baking dish in a microwave set on high for about 1 minute.

• Graham cracker crumbs are easily made in a food processor. It takes about nine sheets of graham crackers (each sheet has four individual crackers) to make 1¼ cups of crumbs.

18 bars

2 • Cakes

Devil's Food Cake

How did this cake earn its name? Was it because the cake was so rich, it tasted like sin to our grandmothers? Some writers hold that theory and propose that some wag named devil's food cake to contrast with angel food cake, an earlier creation. Another theory suggests that devil's food is a cake leavened by baking soda, and when the soda interacts with cocoa, it gives a reddish tint to the cake, hence the association with the devil. Some recipes in the 1950s called for adding an entire bottle of red food coloring to the batter to enhance the red tint. We have made the cake with and without the food coloring and think the color change is so subtle that it is not worth the bother. The first printed recipe for devil's food cake appeared around 1905.

Cake

2½ cups sifted unbleached all-purpose flour

⅔ cup unsweetened cocoa powder

1 tablespoon baking soda

¼ teaspoon salt

½ cup (1 stick) butter, at room temperature

1⅔ cups sugar

5 large eggs

1⅓ cups buttermilk or plain yogurt

1 teaspoon pure vanilla extract

1. Preheat the oven to 350°F. Grease and flour two 9-inch round cake pans. Line the bottoms with parchment paper or aluminum foil. Grease again, then sprinkle with flour to coat. Shake out any excess flour. Set aside.

2. Sift together the flour, cocoa, baking soda, and salt. Set aside.

3. In a large mixing bowl, beat the butter until creamy. Gradually add the sugar and beat until fluffy. Add the eggs, one at a time, beating well after each addition.

4. Add the flour mixture to the egg mixture alternately with the buttermilk and beat until smooth. Mix in the vanilla. Pour the batter into the prepared pans.

5. Bake for 30 to 35 minutes, until a cake tester inserted in the center of the cake comes out clean.

6. Cool on wire racks for about 10 minutes. Remove the cakes from the pans and cool completely.

Fudge Frosting

4 ounces semisweet chocolate

4 tablespoons butter

4 cups confectioners' sugar, sifted

½ cup milk, or more as needed

1 teaspoon pure vanilla extract

⅛ teaspoon salt

7. To make the frosting, combine the chocolate and butter in a small saucepan. Melt over very low heat, stirring constantly.

8. In a mixing bowl, combine the confectioners' sugar, milk, vanilla, and salt. Beat until well combined. Add the chocolate mixture and beat until smooth. If the frosting is too thick, thin with a little more milk added a teaspoon at a time. If the frosting is too thin, allow it to stand for a few minutes, stirring occasionally. Once it is the right consistency, work quickly because the frosting becomes hard on standing.

10 to 12 servings

cake chemistry 101

Cake batters that use baking soda for leavening require an acid ingredient. When heat is applied, the acid activates the baking soda, causing it to release bubbles of carbon dioxide, which raise the cake. The acid can be supplied by buttermilk, yogurt, or sour milk, interchangeably. Buttermilk and yogurt are both dairy products made by culturing sweet milk with friendly bacteria. Sour milk is made at home by adding 1 teaspoon of lemon juice or vinegar to 1 cup of milk at room temperature, then setting it aside for 15 minutes.

Chocolate Zucchini Cake

Zucchini, originally a New World squash, was popular in Italy for decades before it reached mainstream American kitchens. In the 1960s, zucchini was adopted by American gardeners, who were thrilled with this easy-to-grow vegetable. But "easy-to-grow" soon gave way to "overabundant," and recipes for using up overgrown squash were immediately adopted. The zucchini disappears in this orange-scented cake, but the sneaky vegetable lends its moisture to the texture of the cake and keeps it fresh-tasting for several days longer than most cakes. This cake recipe was developed with Renee Shepherd for *Renee's Garden Recipes*.

2 cups sifted unbleached all-purpose flour

⅓ cup unsweetened cocoa powder

1 teaspoon baking powder

1 teaspoon baking soda

½ teaspoon ground cinnamon

½ teaspoon salt

1¾ cups sugar

½ cup vegetable oil

2 teaspoons finely grated orange zest

1 whole large egg

3 large egg whites, slightly beaten

2 cups finely shredded raw zucchini (do not peel)

⅓ cup buttermilk or plain yogurt, at room temperature

1 teaspoon pure vanilla extract

½ cup (3 ounces) semisweet chocolate chips

Sifted confectioners' sugar

1. Preheat the oven to 350°F. Grease and flour a 10-inch springform pan.

2. Sift together the flour, cocoa, baking powder, baking soda, cinnamon, and salt. Sift together two more times. Set aside.

3. In a large mixing bowl, combine the sugar, oil, and orange zest, mixing well. Add the whole egg and egg whites, one at a time, beating well after each addition. Stir in the zucchini.

4. Combine the buttermilk and vanilla.

5. Add the flour mixture to the egg mixture alternately with the buttermilk, and beat until the batter is smooth. Stir in the chocolate chips, mixing just until combined. Pour the batter into the prepared pan.

6. Bake for 30 to 40 minutes, until a cake tester inserted in the center of the cake comes out clean.

7. Cool on a wire rack for about 10 minutes.

8. Run a thin knife around the edge of the springform pan, between the pan and the cake. Set aside for about 30 minutes, or until cool. Then remove the sides of the pan.

9. When the cake is completely cool, sprinkle with confectioners' sugar.

10 to 12 servings

Take forty eggs and divide the whites from the yolks, and beat them to a froth.

Then work four pounds of butter to a cream, and put the whites of the eggs to it, a tablespoonful at a time, until it is well worked.

Then put four pounds of sugar, finely powdered, to it in the same manner.

Then put in the yolks of eggs and five pounds of flour and five pounds of fruit.

Two hours will bake it.

Add to it one-half an ounce of mace, one nutmeg, one-half pint of wine and some French brandy.

This was made by Martha Custis for her grandmama.

— "How to Make a Great Cake," from *Mrs. Colquitt's Savannah Cook Book;* the recipe itself was copied from an older manuscript dated Mount Vernon, 1781

German Chocolate Cake

One would think that this cake has its origins in Germany or with German settlers in Pennsylvania or the Midwest, but it isn't so. It seems that when Walter Baker, grandson of the founder of Baker's chocolate, teamed up with a gentleman named German, they created a sweet baking chocolate such as the one used here. This cake owes its name to the "German" chocolate that is used in the recipe. The original recipe was printed on a box of German sweet chocolate.

Although you can use just about any frosting for this cake, coconut pecan frosting is traditional.

6 ounces dark sweet chocolate, cut into small pieces

½ cup water

2⅓ cups sifted cake flour

1 teaspoon baking soda

½ teaspoon salt

1 cup (2 sticks) butter, at room temperature

1¾ cups sugar

4 large eggs, separated

1 teaspoon pure vanilla extract

1 cup buttermilk or plain yogurt

¼ teaspoon cream of tartar

Coconut Pecan Frosting (page 101)

1. Preheat the oven to 350°F. Lightly grease three 9-inch round cake pans. Line the bottoms with parchment paper or aluminum foil. Grease again, then sprinkle with flour to coat. Shake out any excess flour. Set aside.

2. Combine the chocolate and water and melt over very low heat, stirring until smooth. Set aside to cool.

3. Sift together the flour, baking soda, and salt. Set aside.

4. In a large mixing bowl, beat the butter until creamy. Gradually add 1½ cups of the sugar, beating until fluffy. Add the egg yolks, one at a time, beating well after each addition. Blend in the melted chocolate and the vanilla. Add the flour mixture alternately with the buttermilk, mixing just until the batter is smooth and blended.

5. In another bowl, beat the egg whites until foamy. Add the cream of tartar and beat until soft peaks form. Add the remaining ¼ cup of sugar gradually and beat until stiff but not dry. The egg whites should hold their shape and remain moist. Stir one quarter of the egg whites into the batter, then gently fold in the remainder. Spoon the batter into the prepared pans.

6. Bake for 30 to 35 minutes, until a cake tester inserted in the center of the cake comes out clean.

7. Cool on wire racks for 10 minutes. Remove the cakes from the pans and cool completely.

8. Frost with the Coconut Pecan Frosting.

10 to 12 servings

Let all things be done decently and in order and the first thing to put in order when you are going to bake is yourself. Secure the hair in a net or other covering, to prevent any from falling, and brush the shoulders and back to be sure none are lodged there and might blow off; make the hands and fingernails clean, roll the sleeves up above the elbows, and put on a large clean apron. Clean the kitchen table of utensils and everything not needed, and provide everything that will be needed until the cake is baked, not forgetting even the broom-splints previously picked off a new broom and laid away carefully in a little box. (A knitting needle may be kept for testing cake instead of splints.)

If it is warm weather, place the eggs in cold water, and let stand for a few minutes, as they will then make a finer froth; and be sure they are fresh, as they will not make a stiff froth from any amount of beating if old. The cake-tins should be prepared before the cake, when baking powder is used, as it effervesces but once, and there should be no delay in baking, as the mixture should be made firm by the heat, while the effervescing process is going on.

— Mrs. Florence K. Stanton, *The Practical Housekeeper* (Philadelphia: Keeler & Kirkpatrick, 1898)

Chocolate Layer Cake

Theobroma — "food of the gods" — is the Latin name for chocolate. Can a birthday party be complete without a chocolate layer cake? This is a dark, moist cake with a tender texture.

3 ounces unsweetened chocolate

2 cups sifted cake flour

1 teaspoon baking soda

½ teaspoon salt

6 tablespoons butter, at room temperature

1½ cups sugar

2 large eggs

1 teaspoon pure vanilla extract

¾ cup milk

½ cup sour cream

Chocolate Frosting (page 98)

8 walnut halves, to garnish (optional)

1. Preheat the oven to 350°F. Lightly grease two 8-inch round cake pans. Line the bottoms with parchment paper or aluminum foil. Grease again, then sprinkle with flour to coat. Shake out any excess flour. Set aside.

2. Melt the chocolate over very low heat or in a microwave. Stir until smooth. Set aside to cool.

3. Sift together the flour, baking soda, and salt. Set aside.

4. In a large mixing bowl, beat the butter until creamy. Gradually add the sugar, beating until fluffy. Add the eggs, one at a time, beating well after each addition. Blend in the chocolate and vanilla. Add the flour mixture alternately with the milk and sour cream, mixing just until the batter is smooth and blended. Spoon the batter into the prepared pans.

5. Bake for 30 to 35 minutes, until a cake tester inserted in the center of the cake comes out clean.

6. Cool on wire racks for about 10 minutes. Remove the cakes from the pans and cool completely.

7. Frost with the Chocolate Frosting. Garnish with the walnut halves (if using).

8 servings

Pound Cake

In the days before our heavy reliance on cookbooks, many cakes were reduced to easily remembered formulas. A one-two-three-four cake required 1 cup butter, 2 cups sugar, 3 cups flour, and 4 eggs. Likewise, the pound cake has an easily remembered formula: 1 pound (2 cups) butter, 1 pound (2 cups) sugar, 1 pound (4 cups) flour, and 1 pound (about 9) eggs. Those proportions make two 9-inch loaves or a single 10-inch tube cake. We don't follow those exact proportions anymore because our ingredients have changed. Butter has more fat and less water than it used to; flour, too, is less moist; and sugar is cleaner and therefore sweeter. This variation on the "half-pound" cake delivers good old-fashioned taste and a dense, velvety texture.

2 cups unbleached all-purpose flour

¼ teaspoon salt

1 cup (2 sticks) butter, at room temperature

1¾ cups granulated sugar

5 large eggs

1½ teaspoons vanilla extract or 1 tablespoon finely grated lemon zest and 1 tablespoon lemon juice

Sifted confectioners' sugar, to garnish

1. Preheat the oven 325°F. Lightly grease and flour a 9- by 5-inch loaf pan. Set aside.

2. Sift together the flour and salt. Set aside.

3. In the large bowl of an electric mixer, beat the butter until very light and creamy. Add the granulated sugar gradually and continue beating for 5 minutes, until the mixture is very fluffy. Beat in the eggs, one at a time, beating well after each addition. Add the vanilla. Fold in the flour mixture, mixing just until the batter is smooth and blended. Spoon the batter into the prepared pan.

4. Bake for 1 hour 15 minutes, or until a cake tester inserted in the center of the cake comes out clean.

5. Cool on a wire rack for about 10 minutes. Remove the cake from the pan and cool completely.

6. Sprinkle with the confectioners' sugar.

12 servings

Coconut Cake

Baking with coconut got a big boost when Franklin Baker accepted a cargo of coconuts from Cuba in lieu of cash for a shipment of flour to Havana. When he found it difficult to market the whole nuts, he bought machinery and developed a method of making the flaked coconut we are accustomed to purchasing in plastic bags. As a convenience food, coconut was readily adopted by American bakers, who turned it into delicious cream pies and layer cakes, such as this one.

We are among those who believe that every good cake deserves a little chocolate. So this snowy white cake is filled with a chocolate buttercream between the layers. Billowy clouds of lemony buttercream and toasted coconut make a luscious topping for this three-layer cake.

Cake

3 cups cake flour	½ cup white solid vegetable shortening
4 teaspoons baking powder	1¾ cups sugar
1 teaspoon salt	6 egg whites
½ teaspoon cream of tartar	1⅓ cups coconut or regular milk
1 cup flaked sweetened coconut	1½ teaspoons coconut extract
½ cup butter (1 stick), at room temperature	1½ teaspoons lemon extract

1. Preheat the oven to 350°F. Grease and flour three 8-inch cake pans. Line the bottoms with parchment paper or aluminum foil. Grease again, then sprinkle with flour to coat. Shake out any excess flour. Set aside.

2. Sift together the flour, baking powder, salt, and cream of tartar into a medium-sized mixing bowl. Sift two more times. Stir in the coconut.

3. In the large bowl of an electric mixer, cream the butter and shortening. Gradually add the sugar and beat for 5 minutes.

4. In a large mixing bowl, beat the egg whites with a fork or whisk for 1 minute. Add the coconut milk and beat until well blended.

5. Add one third of the flour mixture and one third of the egg whites to the butter and shortening mixture. Beat until well blended. Continue adding the flour mixture and egg whites in thirds until all is combined. Add the coconut and lemon extracts and beat for about 1 minute, until well combined. The batter will be thick. Spoon the batter into the prepared cake pans and smooth the tops.

6. Bake for 25 to 35 minutes, rotating the pans in the oven after 20 minutes for even baking, until a tester inserted into the center comes out clean.

7. Cool on wire racks for about 10 minutes. Remove the cakes from the pans and cool completely.

(frosting recipe on next page)

fresh coconuts

The flavor of fresh coconut is far superior to that of the dried packaged flakes. To prepare a fresh coconut: Pierce two of the eyes with a strong, sharp instrument, such as a metal skewer or ice pick. Shake out the juice. Smell it for rancidity. If it tastes and smells fresh, serve it in a drink; otherwise, discard the juice. The flesh will be fine regardless of the state of the juice.

Bake the empty nut in a 400°F oven for 15 minutes. Lay the hot nut on a table or counter and give it a sharp blow with a hammer right at the center of the shell. It will break cleanly in two. Pare away the brown skin with a sharp knife and grate the white flesh in a food processor.

Buttercream Frosting

1 cup sweetened flaked coconut

½ cup plus 2 tablespoons unsalted butter, at room temperature

5 cups confectioners' sugar, sifted

Pinch of salt

4 to 5 tablespoons half-and-half or light cream

1 teaspoon lemon or pure vanilla extract

1½ ounces unsweetened chocolate, melted

8. To make the frosting, preheat the oven to 300°F. Spread the coconut on a baking sheet and toast for 5 to 10 minutes. Watch carefully and shake the pan from time to time. Once the coconut begins browning, it will scorch quite easily. Remove from the hot pan and set it aside to cool.

9. Whip the butter with an electric mixer until light and fluffy. Add half the sugar and the salt and beat until combined. Add the remaining sugar and 3 tablespoons of the half-and-half. Beat until very smooth, adding more half-and-half as needed for a good spreading consistency.

10. Remove about three quarters of the buttercream to a bowl. Mix in the lemon flavoring and set aside. To the remaining buttercream, beat in the chocolate until smooth.

11. Spread the chocolate buttercream between the cake layers. Cover the top and sides with the white buttercream, swirling the frosting to make swirls and peaks. Sprinkle the toasted coconut on top.

10 to 12 servings

Banana Cake

The Koran says the forbidden fruit in the Garden of Eden was a banana, not an apple. Bananas were cultivated in India at least as far back as 2000 B.C. Alexander the Great found the wise men of India eating bananas when he crossed the Indus in 327 B.C., hence the banana's botanical name, *Musa sapientum,* "of the wise muse."

2 cups sifted unbleached all-purpose flour

1 teaspoon baking powder

1 teaspoon baking soda

½ teaspoon salt

⅛ teaspoon freshly grated nutmeg

½ cup (1 stick) butter or vegetable shortening, at room temperature

1½ cups sugar

2 large eggs

1 teaspoon pure vanilla extract

1¼ cups mashed ripe bananas

⅔ cup buttermilk or plain yogurt

½ cup toasted chopped walnuts (optional)

Chocolate Frosting (page 98), Vanilla Frosting (page 99), or Sea Foam Frosting (page 102)

1. Preheat the oven to 350°F. Lightly grease two 9-inch round cake pans. Line the bottoms with parchment paper or aluminum foil. Grease again, then sprinkle with flour to coat. Shake out any excess flour. Set aside.

2. Sift together the flour, baking powder, baking soda, salt, and nutmeg. Set aside.

3. In a large mixing bowl, beat the butter until creamy. Gradually add the sugar, beating until fluffy. Add the eggs, one at a time, beating well after each addition. Add the vanilla. Add the flour mixture alternately with the bananas and buttermilk, mixing just until batter is smooth and blended. Fold in the chopped nuts (if using). Spoon the batter into the prepared pans.

4. Bake for 25 to 30 minutes, until a cake tester inserted in the center of the cake comes out clean.

5. Cool on wire racks for about 10 minutes. Remove the cakes from the pans and cool completely.

6. Frost with Chocolate Frosting, Vanilla Frosting, or Sea Foam Frosting.

10 to 12 servings

Lady Baltimore Cake

A largely forgotten 1906 romance novel by Owen Wister entitled *Lady Baltimore* is responsible for spreading the fame of this cake. Mr. Wister enjoyed the cake at the Lady Baltimore Tea Room in Charleston, South Carolina, and lovingly described the cake in his book. With its filling of sherry-soaked dried fruits and nuts, the cake is at least as memorable as Mr. Wister's prose.

Cake

2½ cups sifted cake flour

2½ teaspoons baking powder

½ teaspoon salt

½ cup (1 stick) butter, at room temperature

1¼ cups plus 1 tablespoon sugar

1 teaspoon pure vanilla extract

1 cup milk, at room temperature

4 large egg whites, at room temperature

¼ teaspoon cream of tartar

1. Preheat the oven to 350°F. Grease and flour two 8-inch round cake pans. Line the pans with parchment paper or aluminum foil. Grease again, then sprinkle with flour to coat. Shake out any excess flour. Set aside.

2. Sift together the flour, baking powder, and salt. Sift two more times. Set aside.

3. In a large mixing bowl, beat the butter until creamy. Gradually add 1¼ cups of the sugar and the vanilla. Beat until fluffy. Add the flour mixture alternately with the milk, mixing just until the batter is smooth and blended.

4. In another bowl, beat the egg whites until foamy. Add the cream of tartar and beat until soft peaks form. Add the remaining 1 tablespoon of sugar gradually, and beat until the egg whites are stiff but not dry. The egg whites should hold their shape and remain moist. Stir one quarter of the egg whites into the batter, then gently fold in the remainder. Spoon the batter into the prepared pans.

5. Bake for 25 to 30 minutes, until a cake tester inserted in the center of the cake comes out clean.

6. Cool on wire racks for 10 minutes. Remove the cakes from the pans and cool completely.

Filling and Frosting

½ cup chopped raisins
⅓ cup finely chopped dried cherries
⅓ cup finely chopped moist figs

¼ cup sherry
½ cup chopped pecans
Seven-Minute Frosting (page 99)

7. While the cake cools, make the filling. In a medium-sized bowl, combine the raisins, cherries, and figs with the sherry. Set aside.

8. Prepare Seven-Minute Frosting according to the recipe directions.

9. Drain off the excess liquid from the dried fruits. Stir in the pecans. Fold one third of the frosting into the filling mixture and mix until combined evenly.

10. Spread the filling between the two cake layers. Spread the remaining frosting over the top and sides of the cake.

10 to 12 servings

cake flour for tender cakes

Cake flour produces cakes that are lighter and more tender than cakes made with all-purpose flour. Cake flour is high in starch and low in protein (gluten), which enables it to blend more easily into a batter. If you don't have cake flour on hand, you can make a substitute with all-purpose flour and cornstarch. Just sift together 3 parts all-purpose flour to 1 part cornstarch.

Spice Cake

A cup of cappuccino and a frosty fall afternoon do justice to this moist, light spice cake. The coffee-flavored whipped cream is just the right complement to the lively combination of spices.

Cake

2¼ cups unbleached all-purpose flour

1½ teaspoons baking powder

1½ teaspoons ground cinnamon

1 teaspoon baking soda

½ teaspoon ground ginger

½ teaspoon fleshly grated nutmeg

½ teaspoon salt

¼ teaspoon ground allspice

¼ teaspoon ground cloves

½ cup (1 stick) butter or vegetable shortening, at room temperature

1 cup granulated sugar

½ cup firmly packed dark brown sugar

2 large eggs

1 teaspoon pure vanilla extract

1 cup buttermilk, plain yogurt, or sour milk

1. Preheat the oven to 350°F. Lightly grease two 8-inch round cake pans. Line the bottoms with parchment paper or aluminum foil. Grease again, then sprinkle with flour to coat. Shake out any excess flour. Set aside.

2. Sift together the flour, baking powder, cinnamon, baking soda, ginger, nutmeg, salt, allspice, and cloves. Set aside.

3. In a large mixing bowl, beat the butter until creamy. Gradually add the granulated and brown sugars, beating until fluffy. Add the eggs, one at a time, beating well after each addition. Add the vanilla. Add the flour mixture alternately with the buttermilk, mixing just until the batter is smooth and blended. Divide the batter between the prepared pans.

4. Bake for 30 minutes, or until a cake tester inserted in the center of the cake comes out clean. Cool on wire racks for about 10 minutes. Remove the cakes from the pans and cool completely.

Coffee Whipped Cream

1 cup heavy whipping cream

1 tablespoon instant coffee powder

¼ cup sifted confectioners' sugar

½ teaspoon pure vanilla extract

5. To make the whipped cream, combine the heavy whipping cream and coffee powder in a large bowl. Refrigerate for 15 minutes. Beat until soft peaks form. Add the confectioners' sugar and vanilla and beat until stiff.

6. Spread the cream between the layers and over the top and sides of the cake. Keep the frosted cake refrigerated.

NOTE: To make sour milk, add 1 teaspoon of lemon juice or vinegar to 1 cup of milk (at room temperature). Set aside for 15 minutes.

8 servings

stack cakes

One type of cake you don't see very often anymore is a stack cake, a kind of pioneer potluck cake. Guests invited to a wedding would each bring a cake layer — any flavor — to make the wedding cake. The layers were held together by applesauce. A bride's popularity was gauged by the number of stacks and their heights.

Boston Cream Pie

How did a dessert that is so clearly a cake come to be named a pie? No one seems to know. Boston cream pie was on the menu when the famed Parker House in Boston opened its doors in 1856, but at the time it was called a Parker House chocolate pie. The Parker House really should get the credit not for inventing this delectable dessert, but for adding the chocolate glaze topping. Cakes with a cream filling between the layers (sometimes called cream cakes or pudding-cake pies) do exist in earlier cookbooks, as does the Washington pie, a cake similar to Boston cream pie but filled with raspberry jam instead of pastry cream.

Cake Layers

1½ cups sifted cake flour	1⅓ cups sugar
1½ teaspoons baking powder	1½ teaspoons pure vanilla extract
¼ teaspoon salt	2 tablespoons butter
3 large eggs	¾ cup hot (not boiling) milk

1. To make the cake, preheat the oven to 350°F. Lightly grease two 8-inch round cake pans. Line the bottoms of the pans with parchment paper or aluminum foil. Grease again, then sprinkle with flour to coat. Shake out any excess flour. Set aside.

2. Sift together the flour, baking powder, and salt. Sift two more times. Return the flour mixture to the sieve and set aside.

3. In the large bowl of an electric mixer, beat the eggs for 3 to 4 minutes, until thick and lemon colored. Gradually add the sugar and beat for another 5 minutes (by hand, beat for 8 minutes). Add the vanilla, mixing until blended.

4. Melt the butter in the hot milk. Pour the hot milk into the egg mixture all at once. The batter will be thin.

5. Sift half the flour mixture into the batter and quickly fold it in. Repeat with the second half of the flour. The folding in of the milk and flour mixture should take only about 1 minute. Divide the batter between the prepared pans.

6. Bake for 20 to 25 minutes, until a cake tester inserted in the center of the cake comes out clean.

7. Cool on wire racks for about 10 minutes. Remove the cakes from the pans and cool completely.

Pastry Cream Filling

¼ cup sugar

2½ tablespoons unbleached all-purpose flour

¼ teaspoon salt

1 cup hot (not boiling) milk or half-and-half

3 large egg yolks, lightly beaten

1 teaspoon pure vanilla extract

1 tablespoon butter, cut into small pieces

8. To prepare the pastry cream filling, in a heavy-bottomed saucepan combine the sugar, flour, and salt. Add the hot milk gradually, stirring constantly with a wire whisk to remove any lumps. Cook over medium-high heat, stirring constantly, until the mixture is bubbly. Cook and stir for 2 minutes, until it begins to thicken. Remove from the heat.

9. Stir a few teaspoonfuls of the hot mixture at a time into the egg yolks, beating constantly until well blended. Return the egg yolk mixture to the saucepan. Stir and cook for 2 minutes longer, until thick and smooth. Remove from the heat.

10. Add the vanilla. Gradually stir in the butter. Cover the surface of the pastry cream with plastic. When the pastry cream is cool, refrigerate.

(recipe continued on next page)

Chocolate Glaze

⅔ cup (4 ounces) semisweet chocolate chips
3 tablespoons milk
1 tablespoon butter

1 cup sifted confectioners' sugar
1 teaspoon pure vanilla extract

11. To make the chocolate glaze, in a small saucepan combine the chocolate chips, milk, and butter. Cook over very low heat until melted and smooth. Gradually combine the chocolate mixture with the confectioners' sugar. Stir in the vanilla. Cool until thick enough to spread.

Assembly

12. When the cake is completely cooled, the pastry cream is cold, and the glaze is thick enough to spread, spread the cream between the cake layers and the glaze over the top cake layer.

13. Allow the glaze to set for about 2 hours before serving.

8 servings

cakes through the ages

Cakes predate written history. Archaeological evidence suggests that Neolithic people baked cakes made of crushed grains on hot stones. The Egyptians developed ovens, which made cake making more predictable, though their cakes were still primitive compared with the confections we serve today. The Egyptians and the Greeks used honey-sweetened cakes as offerings to their gods. These cakes were also served at weddings and other special occasions.

Skip ahead to the Romans, whose cakes were flat and heavy and made with barley, raisins, pine nuts, pomegranate seeds, and sweet wine. Cato published a recipe for cheesecake sweetened with honey in his treatise *On Agriculture* in A.D. 75. The Romans introduced the idea of yeast-raised cakes, and for a while there wasn't much difference between cakes and breads.

Cake's name comes from an Old Norse word *kaka,* which in Middle English became *cake.* The saying "You can't have your cake and eat it, too" first appeared in print in 1562 in John Heywood's *Proverbs and Epigrams.* During the Middle Ages, Italian cooks became famous for their baking skills and were often employed by wealthy households in England and France. These cooks are credited with inventing the sponge cake, which was called "biscuit" at the time. The earliest recipe for sponge cake appeared in print in 1615.

In the 1700s, cakes were raised with eggs, often beaten for hours. The batters were sometimes poured into elaborate molds, but more often, cakes were baked in loaf pans. Tea cakes are a direct descendant of those early cakes.

It wasn't until the development of reliable baking soda and baking powder and the availability of modern ovens after 1870 that cakes as we know them today emerged.

Chocolate Marble Cake

Marble cakes — made with molasses, rather than chocolate — were probably the invention of Mennonites from Pennsylvania. The Pennsylvania Dutch were known for their vast range and skill when it came to cooking, and they particularly excelled in dessert making.

2 cups granulated sugar

½ cup unsweetened cocoa powder

¼ cup strong brewed coffee

3 cups sifted cake flour

2 teaspoons baking powder

1 teaspoon baking soda

½ teaspoon salt

¾ cup (1½ sticks) butter, at room temperature

1½ teaspoons pure vanilla extract

4 large eggs

1⅔ cups buttermilk or plain yogurt, at room temperature

Zest of 1 orange, finely grated

Sifted confectioners' sugar, to garnish (optional)

1. Preheat the oven to 350°F. Lightly grease and flour a 9-inch tube or Bundt pan. Set aside.

2. In a medium-sized bowl, mix ¼ cup of the granulated sugar and the cocoa. Add the coffee gradually and stir until blended. Set aside.

3. Sift together the flour, baking powder, baking soda, and salt. Set aside.

4. In a large mixing bowl, beat the butter until creamy. Gradually add the remaining 1¾ cups of sugar and the vanilla, beating until fluffy. Add the eggs, one at a time, beating well after each addition. Add the flour mixture alternately with the buttermilk, mixing just until the batter is smooth and blended.

5. Remove about one third of the batter and add it to the cocoa mixture, blending well.

6. To the remaining batter in the mixing bowl, stir in the orange zest.

7. Using a tablespoon, spoon alternate spoonfuls of the white and chocolate batters into the prepared baking pan. Swirl a spatula through the batter to give a marbled effect.

8. Bake for 55 to 60 minutes, until a cake tester inserted in the center of the cake comes out clean.

9. Cool on a wire rack for about 10 minutes. Run a spatula carefully around the sides and center tube of the pan before turning the cake out onto the rack. The cake should cool right-side up.

10. Sprinkle with confectioners' sugar (if using) just before serving.

10 to 12 servings

judging when a cake is done

An underbaked cake will be dense, overly moist, and sunken in the center. An overbaked cake will be dry. Removing a cake at the perfect moment of doneness is not difficult:

- The cake should shrink slightly from the edges of the pan.
- The cake top should spring back when lightly pressed with a fingertip.
- A cake tester or wooden pick inserted near the center of the cake should come out clean, with no batter or moist crumbs clinging to it.

Applesauce Cake

One of the pleasures of fall is going to a nearby orchard and picking apples. We make a stop at the bin of "drops" for bargain-priced sauce apples, which we cook down, strain, and flavor with cinnamon, no sugar needed. Some of that sauce makes its way into this moist cake.

½ cup dried currants

½ cup raisins

1⅔ cups plus 1 tablespoon sifted unbleached all-purpose flour

1 teaspoon baking powder

1 teaspoon ground cinnamon

½ teaspoon baking soda

½ teaspoon ground cloves

½ teaspoon freshly grated nutmeg

¼ teaspoon salt

½ cup (1 stick) butter, at room temperature

¾ cup granulated sugar

½ cup firmly packed dark brown sugar

2 large eggs

1 teaspoon pure vanilla extract

1 cup thick applesauce, warmed

2 tablespoons milk

Brown Sugar Frosting (page 102)

Chopped peanuts or toasted almonds, to garnish

1. Preheat the oven to 350°F. Lightly grease and flour a 9-inch tube or Bundt pan. Set aside.

2. In a small bowl, toss the currants and raisins with 1 tablespoon of the flour. Set aside.

3. Sift together the remaining 1⅔ cups of flour and the baking powder, cinnamon, baking soda, cloves, nutmeg, and salt. Set aside.

4. In a large mixing bowl, beat the butter until creamy. Gradually add the granulated and brown sugars, beating until fluffy. Add the eggs, one at a time, beating well after each addition. Add the vanilla. Add the flour mixture alternately with the warm applesauce and milk, mixing just until batter is smooth and blended. Fold in the currants and raisins. Spoon the batter into the prepared pan.

5. Bake for 45 to 50 minutes, until a cake tester inserted in the center of the cake comes out clean.

6. Cool on a wire rack for about 10 minutes. Run a spatula carefully around the sides and center tube of the pan before turning out the cake onto the rack. The cake should cool right-side up.

7. Frost with Brown Sugar Frosting when completely cool. Sprinkle with the chopped nuts.

10 to 12 servings

scripture cakes

During the nineteenth century, scripture cakes were popular. Half recipe, half puzzle, each ingredient was listed as a biblical verse and the baker had to decipher its meaning. These recipes exist primarily in handwritten manuscripts and receipt books, handed down in families. This one was found in a book entitled *A Vermont Cookbook by Vermont Cooks* (White River Junction, Vt., 1958).

4 cups I Kings (first part)
1 cup Judges 5:25 (last clause)
2 cups Jeremiah 6:20
2 cups I Samuel 30:12
2 cups Nahum 3:12 (found in the Apocrypha)
1 tablespoon Numbers 17:8
1 large tablespoon I Samuel 14:25
Season to taste of II Chronicles 9:9
6 of Jeremiah 17:11
A pinch of Leviticus 2:13
½ cup Genesis 24:20
2 teaspoons Amos 4:5
Follow Solomon's advice for making good boys, Proverbs 23:14, and you will have a good cake.

Gingerbread

Ginger isn't native to the New World, but it made an early appearance with the English colonists, who frequently made gingerbread. A recipe appeared in Amelia Simmons's *American Cookery* in 1796. A dessert that has stood the test of time, gingerbread to some is the quintessential comfort food — wildly appetizing as it bakes and fills the house with the warm scent of ginger, richly satisfying to eat, and wonderfully pleasing as an excuse for whipped cream. It's also delicious served with applesauce or rhubarb sauce and vanilla ice cream.

1½ cups sifted unbleached all-purpose flour	½ cup (1 stick) butter, at room temperature
2 teaspoons ground ginger	¾ cup firmly packed dark brown sugar
1 teaspoon baking soda	1 large egg, lightly beaten
¾ teaspoon ground cinnamon	½ cup dark molasses (not blackstrap)
¼ teaspoon ground cloves	½ cup boiling hot brewed coffee
¼ teaspoon salt	Confectioners' sugar, to garnish (optional)

1. Preheat the oven to 350°F. Lightly grease and flour an 8-inch square baking pan. Set aside.

2. Sift together the flour, ginger, baking soda, cinnamon, cloves, and salt. Set aside.

3. In a bowl, beat the butter until creamy. Gradually add the sugar, beating until fluffy. Add the egg and beat until smooth. Beat in the molasses. Add the flour mixture alternately with the coffee, mixing until just combined. The batter will be thin. Pour the batter into the prepared pan.

4. Bake for about 35 minutes, or until a cake tester inserted in the center of the cake comes out clean.

5. Cool on a wire rack.

6. Dust with the confectioners' sugar (if using). To make a special presentation, you can top the gingerbread with a design made from confectioners' sugar. To do so, use a triple thickness of decorative paper doilies. Remove any excess uncut paper. Fasten the doilies to the top of the gingerbread with toothpicks or pins. Sprinkle over and around the doilies with sifted confectioners' sugar. Remove the picks or pins and lift the doilies straight up. There should remain a lacy snowflake design of powdered sugar.

6 to 8 servings

I remember that at one time I saw two of my young mistresses and some lady visitors eating ginger-cakes, in the yard. At that time those cakes seemed to me to be absolutely the most tempting and desirable things I had ever seen and then and there resolved that, if I ever got free, the height of my ambition would be reached if I could get to the point where I could secure and eat ginger-cakes in the way I saw those ladies doing.

— Booker T. Washington, *Up from Slavery*, 1901

Carrot Cake

Those who scoffed at seed-eaters and granola-crunchers were forced to rethink their prejudices when it came to carrot cake. And why did carrot cake become the standard for health-food aficionados? It could have been because the moist cake stands up even to the assault of whole wheat, or perhaps because it is packed with fiber and vitamins and low in animal fats. Perhaps people adopted it because the recipe is so often fool-proof and lends itself to multiplication for huge wedding cakes. Or, perhaps, carrot cake became so universally popular because it tastes so good.

2 cups sifted unbleached all-purpose flour

2 teaspoons baking powder

1½ teaspoons baking soda

1½ teaspoons ground cinnamon

1 teaspoon salt

¼ teaspoon ground allspice

¼ teaspoon freshly grated nutmeg

1 cup vegetable oil

1 cup granulated sugar

¾ cup firmly packed light brown sugar

4 large eggs

1 tablespoon finely grated orange zest

1 teaspoon pure vanilla extract

3 cups lightly packed, finely shredded carrots

8 ounces crushed pineapple, drained

1 cup toasted chopped walnuts

Cream Cheese Frosting (page 100)

Toasted coconut, to garnish (optional)

1. Preheat the oven to 350°F. Lightly grease and flour a 9- by 13-inch baking pan. Set aside.

2. Sift together the flour, baking powder, baking soda, cinnamon, salt, allspice, and nutmeg. Set aside.

3. In a mixing bowl, beat the oil and granulated and brown sugars until thoroughly combined. Add the eggs, one at a time, beating well after each addition. Add the orange zest and vanilla; continue beating until fluffy. Gradually add the flour mixture, mixing just until the batter is smooth and blended. Fold in the carrots, pineapple, and walnuts. Spoon the batter into the prepared pan.

4. Bake for 35 minutes, or until a cake tester inserted in the center of the cake comes out clean.

5. Cool on a wire rack.

6. Frost with Cream Cheese Frosting when completely cool. Sprinkle with the toasted coconut (if using).

12 to 16 servings

the non-fermentation movement

The Temperance Movement of the 1800s had its impact on cake baking, strange though that may sound. One arm of the movement, the religiously inspired Non-Fermentation Movement, wanted to ban the use of yeast in breads and cakes, as yeast produces alcohol in the rising process, albeit in minute amounts. Instead, the use of baking powder, which produces a gas that raises the batter, was promoted. Some manufacturers of baking powder and other "safe, non-fermenting yeasts" also claimed that their products prevented rickets, cholera, and tooth decay while promoting muscle and bone growth. The Non-Fermentation Movement got a boost when agents for Horsford's Self-Raising Bread Preparation distributed for free *The Good Cook's Hand Book* in the 1860s and 1870s, which provided plenty of recipes using baking powder.

nutty facts

The world's two most popular walnut varieties are the black walnut and the English walnut. Black walnuts are native to the eastern part of the United States, where they grow on trees that stand more than 100 feet tall. English walnuts originated in Persia, though both walnut varieties are now grown in temperate zones all over the world. Black walnut shells are very strong and more difficult to crack than English walnut shells. Also, black walnuts are much more strongly flavored than English walnuts; in fact, some people prefer to use half English walnuts and half black walnuts in their recipes to subdue the flavor.

Toasting walnuts enhances their flavor. To toast walnuts, place them in a dry skillet over medium heat and toast until fragrant, about 5 minutes, shaking the pan occasionally. Or place them in a shallow pan, such as a pie tin, and toast in the oven at 350°F for 7 to 10 minutes. Store walnuts in a cool, dry place. In their shells, walnuts keep for up to 3 months. Shelled walnuts may be placed in an airtight container and refrigerated for up to 6 months. Walnuts can also be frozen for up to a year.

Since 1955, thousands of Americans have gathered each October to celebrate the black walnut harvest at the Black Walnut Festival in Spencer, West Virginia. During the 4-day celebration, some 13 tons of walnuts are hulled and consumed, as visitors enjoy parades, majorette competitions, gospel singers, black powder shoots, road races, antique car shows, and more. The highlight of the event is the black walnut bake-off. For more information, contact the West Virginia Black Walnut Festival (see Resources, page 198).

Black Walnut Cake

If you grew up in the Midwest, particularly Kansas, you might have especially fond memories of this rich, crunchy, moist cake studded with black walnuts. If you don't live near a source of black walnuts, by all means substitute toasted English walnuts.

2¾ cups sifted cake flour

2½ teaspoons baking powder

¾ teaspoon salt

⅔ cup (about 1⅓ sticks) butter, at room temperature

1 cup granulated sugar

⅔ cup firmly packed dark brown sugar

3 large eggs

1 teaspoon pure vanilla extract

1 cup milk

1½ cups finely chopped black walnuts or toasted English walnuts

Burnt Sugar Icing (page 100)

½ cup walnut halves, to garnish

1. Preheat the oven to 350°F. Lightly grease and flour a 9- by 13-inch pan. Set aside.

2. Sift together the flour, baking powder, and salt. Set aside.

3. In a large mixing bowl, beat the butter until creamy. Gradually add the granulated and brown sugars, beating until fluffy. Add the eggs, one at a time, beating well after each addition. Add the vanilla. Add the flour mixture alternately with the milk, mixing just until the batter is smooth and blended. Fold in the nuts. Spoon the batter into the prepared pan.

4. Bake for 30 to 35 minutes, until a cake tester inserted in the center of the cake comes out clean.

5. Cool on a wire rack.

6. Frost with the Burnt Sugar Icing when completely cool. Garnish with the walnut halves.

12 to 16 servings

Poppy Seed Cake

Cookbooks are always advising the reader that fresh is better, and in the case of poppy seeds, this advice is especially true. Consider growing a patch of Oriental poppies and tasting the difference. And the sight of the delicate flowers swaying in the wind is a bonus.

1 cup poppy seeds	2 cups granulated sugar
1 cup milk	2 tablespoons cream sherry
3 cups sifted cake flour	2 teaspoons pure vanilla extract
2½ teaspoons baking powder	6 large egg whites, at room temperature
½ teaspoon salt	¼ teaspoon cream of tartar
1 cup (2 sticks) butter, at room temperature	Sifted confectioners' sugar, to garnish

1. Combine the poppy seeds and milk and let stand for several hours or overnight. Or, if pressed for time, combine the poppy seeds with warm milk and set aside for 1 hour.

2. Preheat the oven to 350°F. Lightly grease and flour a 10-inch tube or Bundt pan or two 9- by 5-inch loaf pans. Set aside.

3. Sift together the flour, baking powder, and salt. Set aside.

4. In a large mixing bowl, beat the butter until creamy, then gradually add 1¾ cups of the granulated sugar, beating until fluffy. Mix in the sherry and vanilla. Add the flour mixture alternately with the poppy seed–milk mixture, mixing just until the batter is smooth and blended.

5. In another bowl, beat the egg whites until foamy. Add the cream of tartar and beat until soft peaks form. Add the remaining ¼ cup of granulated sugar gradually. Beat until stiff but not dry. The egg whites should hold their shape and remain moist. Stir one quarter of the egg whites into the batter, then gently fold in the remainder. Spoon the batter into the prepared pan(s).

6. Bake tube or Bundt cake for 50 to 60 minutes, or bake loaf pans for 40 to 50 minutes, until a cake tester inserted in the center of the cake comes out clean.

7. Cool on a wire rack for about 10 minutes. Remove the cake from the pan and cool completely.

8. Sprinkle with the confectioners' sugar.

10 to 12 servings

But pleasures are like poppies spread
You seize the flower, its bloom is shed;
Or like the snow falls in the river
A moment white, then melts forever.

— Robert Burns, "Tam o' Shanter"

Angel Food Cake

A great, billowy cloud of a cake, yes. But surely not invented by angels? More than one story is attached to the origins of this celestial dessert.

The most credible story is that it was invented by a frugal Pennsylvania Dutch cook who sought to use up egg whites left from the making of egg noodles. Another story credits an Indian cook who somehow sent the recipe to the United States. The recipe wound up in the hands of a baker who baked the cakes behind shuttered windows to prevent competitors from stealing the recipe. At this time, the cake was also known as "mystery cake." Still another story sets down St. Louis as the location of the divine inspiration that led a certain Mr. Sides to make the cake with a secret recipe, which he sold for $25. The catch was that the cake could be made only with a secret white powder, which Mr. Sides also sold. The secret white powder was shortly revealed to be cream of tartar, which whitened the cake and made it tender, and soon the dish was seen on restaurant menus throughout St. Louis, a secret no longer.

1¼ cups sifted cake flour

1½ cups sifted granulated sugar

1¾ cups (12 to 14) egg whites, at room temperature

1¼ teaspoons cream of tartar

¼ teaspoon salt

1 teaspoon pure vanilla extract

½ teaspoon almond extract

Sifted confectioners' sugar, to garnish

1. Preheat the oven to 300°F. Set out a 10-inch tube or angel cake pan. Do not grease.

2. Sift the flour with ½ cup of the granulated sugar. Sift three more times. Set aside.

3. In the large bowl of an electric mixer, beat the egg whites until foamy. Add the cream of tartar and salt and beat until soft peaks form. Continue beating the egg whites until stiff but not dry. The egg whites should hold their shape and remain moist.

4. Beat in the remaining 1 cup of granulated sugar, 1 tablespoon at a time and beating well after each addition, until stiff peaks form. Beat in the vanilla and almond extracts.

5. Sift the flour mixture over the egg whites, about one quarter of it at a time. Using a rubber spatula or flat wire whisk, fold in the flour gently as you rotate the bowl. Continue folding in the flour by quarters until it is all incorporated.

6. Carefully spoon the batter into the ungreased pan. Pass a knife through the batter, going around the pan twice to break up any air bubbles. Smooth the top.

7. Bake for 50 to 60 minutes, until the cake is golden brown and the top springs back when gently pressed.

8. Invert the cake in the pan and let it cool upside down for 1 to 2 hours. If the pan doesn't have feet, you'll have to rig up something to enable the air to circulate freely under the cake. We recommend resting the tube opening on the neck of a glass beverage bottle or funnel.

9. When the cake is completely cool, run a thin spatula around the sides of the pan and center tube. Tap the bottom and sides of the pan to release the cake. Invert the cake and turn it out onto a platter. Sprinkle with the confectioners' sugar.

VARIATION

For a more elaborate presentation, horizontally slice the angel cake into three layers. Spread each layer with crushed sweetened strawberries or drained crushed pineapple. Cover with whipped cream, then coat the sides of the cake with whipped cream.

10 to 12 servings

Many families have owed their prosperity full as much to the propriety of female management, as to the knowledge and activity of the father.

— *Mrs. J. S. Bradley's Housekeeper's Guide*
(Cincinnati: H. M. Rulison, 1853)

Sponge Cake

Few people regard sponge cake as an end in itself, but rather as the base for a luscious layering of cake, fruit, and cream. You can use sponge cake in trifles with custard and fruit, smother it under fresh summer berries, or marry it to ice cream. This cake is light, airy, and golden yellow.

1½ cups sifted cake flour

1½ teaspoons baking powder

½ teaspoon salt

½ cup (about 8) egg yolks

1½ cups granulated sugar

6 tablespoons boiling water

1 tablespoon lemon juice or 1½ teaspoons pure vanilla extract

1 cup (about 8) egg whites, at room temperature

½ teaspoon cream of tartar

Sifted confectioners' sugar, to garnish

1. Preheat the oven to 325°F. Set out a 10-inch tube or angel food cake pan. Do not grease.

2. Sift together the flour, baking powder, and salt. Sift two more times. Return the mixture to the sieve and set aside.

3. In the large bowl of an electric mixer, beat the egg yolks until thick and lemon colored, about 5 minutes. Gradually add 1¼ cups of the granulated sugar and beat an additional 5 minutes. Continue beating and add the boiling water in a steady stream. Beat until the mixture is light and fluffy. Add the lemon juice.

4. Sift one third of the flour mixture at a time over the egg yolk mixture. Using a rubber spatula, gently fold in the flour as you rotate the bowl. The folding in of the flour should take 2 to 3 minutes. Work carefully to avoid deflating the batter.

5. In another bowl, beat the egg whites until foamy. Add the cream of tartar and beat until soft peaks form. Beat in the remaining ¼ cup of granulated sugar, 1 tablespoon at a time, beating well until the egg whites are stiff but not dry. The egg whites should hold their shape and remain moist.

6. Stir one quarter of the egg whites into the batter, then gently fold in the remainder, just until incorporated. Spoon the batter into the pan.

7. Bake for 50 to 55 minutes, until a cake tester inserted in the center of the cake comes out clean.

8. Immediately invert the pan and let the cake cool upside down in the pan for about 2 hours. If the pan doesn't have feet, you'll have to rig up something to enable the air to circulate freely under the cake. We recommend resting the tube opening on the neck of a glass beverage bottle or funnel.

9. When the cake is completely cool, carefully cut away any crust that is stuck to the tube or rim of the pan. Run a thin spatula around the sides of the pan and center tube. Tap the bottom and sides of the pan to help release the cake. Invert the cake and turn it out onto a platter. Sprinkle with the confectioners' sugar.

10 to 12 servings

The baking is the most critical part of cake making. Test the oven with a piece of white paper. If it turns a light yellow in five minutes, it is ready for sponge cake; if a dark yellow in five minutes it is ready for cup cakes.

– The All-Ways Preferable Cook Book,
compiled by Miss Ada A. Hillier,
prepared for The Malleable Steel Range Mfg. Co.,
South Bend, Indiana (date unknown)

Jelly Roll

Since the mid-1800s, jelly rolls have been a popular dessert. They are made from a thin sponge cake that is spread with jelly (or cream) and then rolled. When sliced, each piece presents an attractive pinwheel pattern. Jelly rolls are sometimes called Swiss rolls.

¾ cup sifted cake flour

1 teaspoon baking powder

¼ teaspoon salt

4 large eggs, separated

¾ cup granulated sugar

1 teaspoon pure vanilla extract

¼ teaspoon cream of tartar

Confectioners' sugar, sifted

10 to 12 ounces raspberry or other jam

1. Preheat the oven to 375°F. Grease a 15½- by 10½- by 1-inch jelly-roll pan. Line with parchment paper or aluminum foil. Grease again, then sprinkle with flour to coat. Shake out any excess flour. Set aside.

2. Sift together the flour, baking powder, and salt. Sift two more times. Set aside.

3. In a large mixing bowl, beat the egg yolks until thick and lemon colored. Gradually add ½ cup of the granulated sugar and beat until fluffy. Blend in the vanilla. Beat for 5 minutes. Stir in half the flour mixture, mixing until blended. Add the remaining flour mixture, mixing until well combined. The batter will be stiff.

4. In another bowl, beat the egg whites until foamy. Add the cream of tartar and beat until soft peaks form. Add the remaining ¼ cup of granulated sugar gradually, and beat until the egg whites are stiff but not dry. The egg whites should hold their shape and remain moist. Stir one quarter of the egg whites into the batter, then gently fold in the remainder. Spoon the batter into the prepared pan, spreading it to the corners of the pan.

5. Bake for 12 to 15 minutes, until the cake is golden and the top of the cake springs back when lightly pressed with a finger.

6. Generously sprinkle a kitchen towel with the confectioners' sugar. Invert the cake onto the towel. Carefully peel off the parchment paper or foil. Cut off any crisp edges. While the cake is still hot, roll it up in the towel from the long side, jelly-roll fashion.

7. Cool the cake, seam-side down, on a wire rack for about 30 minutes.

8. Unroll the cake, remove the towel, and spread the cake with the jam. Roll up, place on a serving platter, and sprinkle with additional confectioners' sugar.

NOTE: To use this sponge cake for Baked Alaska (page 94), prepare the cake in a 9-inch cake pan or springform pan lined with parchment paper or aluminum foil. Lightly grease and flour the liner but not the sides of the pan. Bake at 350°F for 25 to 28 minutes, until a tester inserted in the center of the cake comes out clean and the sides of the cake begin to pull away from the pan. Cool in the pan on a wire rack for about 30 minutes. Then invert the cake onto a foil-lined board or platter.

12 servings

preparing pans for baking

Most of the cake recipes in this book call for greasing a pan, lining the pan with parchment paper or aluminum foil, then greasing and flouring the lining. Although older books may use parchment or waxed paper, we find we get better results with aluminum foil or parchment paper. Reusable silicone liners also will work well.

Although you can use butter for greasing pans, we like using solid vegetable shortening. It is more neutral in flavor, burns at a much higher temperature, and leaves less residue in the pan. After greasing the pan, sprinkle in a tablespoon or more of flour. Shake the pan to distribute the flour, then carefully shake out the excess.

Gold Cake

This is the yellow cake that simply doesn't come out of a box. We give the cake a suggestion of orange flavor. You can highlight the traces of orange with a tangy orange frosting, or, if you hate to miss an opportunity for chocolate, frost with your favorite chocolate frosting. Fresh orange segments arranged in a sunburst pattern make a lovely garnish.

1¾ cups sifted cake flour

2 teaspoons baking powder

¼ teaspoon salt

½ cup (1 stick) butter, at room temperature

1 cup sugar

1 teaspoon finely grated orange zest

1 teaspoon orange juice concentrate, at room temperature, or ½ teaspoon orange extract

8 egg yolks (about ½ cup)

½ cup milk

Chocolate Frosting (page 98) or Orange Frosting (page 101)

1. Preheat the oven to 350°F. Lightly grease two 8-inch round cake pans. Line the bottoms with parchment paper or aluminum foil. Grease again, then sprinkle with flour to coat. Shake out the excess flour.

2. Sift together the flour, baking powder, and salt. Set aside.

3. In a large mixing bowl, beat the butter until creamy, then gradually add the sugar, orange zest, and orange juice concentrate, beating until fluffy.

4. Beat the egg yolks in a small bowl until thick and lemon colored. Add to the butter mixture. (If you are using an electric mixer, add the egg yolks to the butter mixture one at a time, beating thoroughly after each addition.)

5. Add about a quarter of the flour mixture to the creamed mixture, beating until blended, then add a third of the milk. Repeat the procedure, alternating the flour and milk, ending with the flour. Mix just until smooth and blended. Divide the batter between the prepared pans.

6. Bake for 25 to 30 minutes, until a cake tester inserted in the center of the cake comes out clean.

7. Cool on wire racks for about 10 minutes. Remove the cakes from the pans and cool completely.

8. Frost with the Orange Frosting or the Chocolate Frosting.

8 servings

what to do when you don't have the right-size pan

Of course, it's best to use the size pan specified in a recipe, but that isn't always possible. You may substitute another-size pan as long as the cake batter fills it at least 1 inch deep; otherwise, the cake won't rise properly. For most cakes, fill the pans half to two-thirds full. Bundt, tube, and loaf pans may be filled a little higher. If you have too much batter, use the excess to fill muffin tins or custard cups.

Your baking time may need to be adjusted if you're using a different-size pan. Check for doneness by inserting a cake tester into the center of the cake. If it comes out clean, the cake is done. You can double-check by seeing that the cake pulls away from the sides of the pan and springs back when lightly pressed in the center.

Honey Cake

Honey cakes were standard fare at teas given by abolitionists in the early 1800s. They were popular because honey replaced the more common molasses, a sweetener produced by slave labor. Today, honey cake is a traditional dessert on Rosh Hashanah, the Jewish New Year, when honey is eaten in hopes of having a sweet year. The rich honey cake goes well with raw apples dipped in honey, another Jewish New Year tradition.

1 cup dark honey, such as buckwheat

½ cup strong brewed black coffee

2½ cups sifted unbleached all-purpose flour

2 teaspoons baking powder

1 teaspoon ground cinnamon

½ teaspoon ground allspice

½ teaspoon baking soda

½ teaspoon ground ginger

¼ teaspoon salt

⅛ teaspoon ground cloves

3 large eggs

¾ cup firmly packed dark brown sugar

⅓ cup vegetable oil

2 teaspoons finely grated orange zest

½ cup chopped walnuts

2 tablespoons finely chopped candied orange peel (optional)

Sifted confectioners' sugar

1. Preheat the oven to 300°F. Thoroughly grease and flour a 9- by 5-inch loaf pan. Set aside.

2. In a small saucepan, mix together the honey and coffee over moderate heat, stirring until combined. Set aside; cool to lukewarm.

3. Sift together the flour, baking powder, cinnamon, allspice, baking soda, ginger, salt, and cloves. Set aside.

4. In a mixing bowl, beat the eggs and brown sugar until light and fluffy. Gradually add the oil and continue beating until thoroughly blended. Add the orange zest. Add the flour mixture alternately with the honey mixture, mixing just until the batter is smooth and blended. Fold in the nuts and the candied orange peel (if using). Spoon the batter into the prepared pan.

5. Bake for 60 to 65 minutes, until a cake tester inserted in the center of the cake comes out clean.

6. Cool on a wire rack for 10 minutes. Turn the cake out of the pan and cool completely. Wrap the cake in aluminum foil or plastic wrap and let it stand overnight to allow the flavors to intensify. Sprinkle with the confectioners' sugar and cut into very thin slices.

12 servings

honey gathering

In the good old days, the housewife was not only responsible for making the cake, but she had to take the honey from the hive as well. Here, then, is "Method of Taking Honey From Bee Hives Without Killing the Bees," from McCall's *Home Cook Book and General Guide*, compiled by Mrs. Jennie Harlan (New York: The McCall Company, 1890):

"Pour two teaspoonsful of chloroform into a piece of rag, double it twice, and place it on the floor-board of the hive, which must be lifted for the purpose, the entrance-hole being carefully secured. In about two minutes and a half there will be a loud humming, which will soon cease. Let the hive remain in this state for six or seven minutes, making about ten minutes in all. Remove the hive and the greater number of bees will be found lying senseless on the board; there will still be a few clinging to the combs, some of which may be brushed out with a feather. They return to animation in from half an hour to one hour after the operation. This plan possesses a great superiority over the usual mode of brimstoning, the bees being preserved alive; and over the more modern plan of fumigation by puff-ball; it is far less trouble, and the honey does not become tainted with the fumes."

Pineapple Upside-Down Cake

Pineapple upside-down cakes were first mentioned in cookbooks in the 1930s, though they were probably invented much earlier. Some books suggest that the pineapple upside-down cake evolved from an earlier cake that was known as bachelor's bread, which was made by pouring sponge cake batter into a pan lined with thin slices of citron (which probably was a type of melon and not the rarely seen citrus fruit) and almonds. After the cake was baked, it was turned upside down onto a platter. The cake's name was a sly poke at the upside-down nature of the bachelor's life — and the quality of his baking!

Topping

1 can (20 ounces) sliced pineapple	⅔ cup firmly packed dark brown sugar
4 tablespoons butter	16 pecan or walnut halves

1. Preheat the oven to 350°F.

2. To make the topping, drain the pineapple, reserving ⅔ cup of the juice for the cake. Over low heat, melt the butter in a heavy ovenproof 9-inch skillet. Or, if you are using a 9-inch glass cake pan or pie plate, melt the butter in the oven. Sprinkle the brown sugar over the melted butter and spread the mixture evenly over the bottom of the pan. Remove from the heat. Arrange eight pineapple slices over the brown sugar. Fill the centers and spaces between the pineapple with pecan halves placed flat-side up.

Cake

1¼ cups sifted unbleached all-purpose flour	⅔ cup granulated sugar
1½ teaspoons baking powder	1 large egg
¼ teaspoon ground ginger	1 teaspoon pure vanilla extract
¼ teaspoon salt	⅔ cup pineapple juice, reserved from pineapple for Topping
6 tablespoons butter or vegetable shortening, at room temperature	

3. To make the cake, sift together the flour, baking powder, ginger, and salt. Set aside.

4. In a mixing bowl, beat the butter until creamy. Gradually add the sugar, beating until fluffy. Beat in the egg and vanilla. Add the flour mixture alternately with the pineapple juice, mixing just until the batter is smooth and blended. Spoon the cake batter over the pineapple.

5. Bake for 40 to 45 minutes, until a tester inserted in the center of the cake comes out clean.

6. Cool for 5 minutes. Loosen the cake around the edge, then invert onto a serving platter. Serve warm.

8 servings

fresh pineapples

While pineapple canned in its own juice is an exceptionally fine canned fruit, fresh pineapple often has more texture and a sharper flavor. To judge whether a pineapple is ripe, look for bright green leaves. Try pulling out a leaf; if it yields easily, the fruit is ripe. The flesh should also feel slightly soft, and the pineapple should have a distinctive pineapple-y smell.

Strawberry Shortcake

There was a time, not so long ago, when strawberry season marked the beginning of summer, when fresh strawberries could be had from mid-June to mid-July only, and the idea of strawberries in February was unthinkable. If you live in the North, the idea of strawberries in February is still unthinkable. The Cello-packed berries shipped from who-knows-where are as tasteless as last summer's dried flowers. Strawberry shortcake, that quintessential summer dessert, can be enjoyed only when berries are fresh and local. And if there are pink stains on your hands from picking the strawberries yourself, and the berries are still warm from the sun, so much the better.

Strawberries

- 6 cups fresh strawberries
- 3 tablespoons sugar, or to taste
- 1 tablespoon strawberry liqueur or crème de cassis

Shortcake Biscuits

- 2 cups unbleached all-purpose flour
- 1 tablespoon baking powder
- 3 tablespoons granulated sugar
- ½ teaspoon salt
- ½ cup (1 stick) butter, cut into small pieces, or 4 tablespoons butter and 4 tablespoons vegetable shortening
- ⅔ cup milk or half-and-half
- 1 to 2 tablespoons butter, at room temperature

Topping

- 1 cup heavy whipping cream
- 2 tablespoons sifted confectioners' sugar
- ⅛ teaspoon freshly grated nutmeg

1. To prepare the strawberries, set aside six strawberries for a garnish. Into a bowl, slice the remaining berries and sprinkle with 3 tablespoons of sugar and the strawberry liqueur. Toss until thoroughly combined. Cover and refrigerate for several hours, stirring occasionally.

2. To make the biscuits, preheat the oven to 425°F. Lightly grease a baking sheet.

3. Sift together the flour, baking powder, granulated sugar, and salt. In a food processor, with a pastry blender, or with your fingertips, process or cut or rub the butter into the flour mixture until it has the consistency of coarse crumbs. Add the milk all at once. Process or stir with a fork just until the dough comes together.

4. Turn out the dough onto a lightly floured work surface. Knead lightly 12 to 15 times, sprinkling with a little flour if the dough is sticky. Roll out or pat the dough into a rectangle ½-inch thick. Cut into six rounds with a floured 3-inch biscuit cutter or use a knife to cut into squares. Place the biscuits close together on the baking sheet. (The biscuits can be refrigerated for up to 2 hours before baking.)

5. Bake for 15 to 18 minutes, until the biscuits are golden.

6. Cool the biscuits briefly on the baking sheet before transferring them to a wire rack until cool enough to handle.

7. Split each biscuit in half. Coat the bottom layers with a little soft butter and transfer to individual serving plates.

8. To make the topping, whip the cream until stiff, gradually adding the confectioners' sugar and nutmeg as you beat.

9. To assemble the dessert, spoon some of the berries over each buttered biscuit half. Cover the berries with some of the whipped cream. Gently press on the top biscuit half. Spoon the remaining strawberries over the top biscuit half. Finish with another spoonful of whipped cream. Garnish each with a whole strawberry.

6 servings

Praline–Sour Cream Coffee Cake

Mom doesn't have time for morning coffee klatches anymore. The term comes from the German *kaffeeklatsch,* which translates as "coffee gossip." Coffee klatches were informal gatherings over coffee, particularly popular during the 1950s and 1960s. Today, Mom is in the office and hasn't time for mid-morning social gatherings. Still, the need for coffee cakes remains constant — for brunches, office treats, and bake sales. This recipe is a classic.

Cake

2 cups unbleached all-purpose flour
1½ teaspoons baking powder
½ teaspoon baking soda
¼ teaspoon salt
1 cup (2 sticks) butter
2 cups sugar
2 teaspoons pure vanilla extract
2 large eggs
2 cups sour cream

Praline

1 cup chopped pecans
2 tablespoons sugar
2 teaspoons ground cinnamon

1. To make the cake, preheat the oven to 350°F. Thoroughly grease and flour a 9-inch tube or Bundt pan. Set aside.

2. Sift together the flour, baking powder, baking soda, and salt. Set aside.

3. In a mixing bowl, beat the butter until creamy. Gradually add the sugar and the vanilla, beating until fluffy. Add the eggs, one at a time, beating well after each addition. Add the sour cream, mixing until smooth. Fold in the flour mixture and beat just until blended. Be sure to avoid overmixing.

4. To make the praline, combine the pecans, sugar, and cinnamon in a small bowl.

5. Spoon half the batter into the prepared pan. Sprinkle the praline evenly over the batter. Top with the remaining batter. With a knife, cut through the batter to distribute the praline.

6. Bake for 55 to 60 minutes, until a cake tester inserted in the center comes out clean.

7. Cool the coffee cake on a rack for 20 minutes.

8. Run a spatula carefully around the sides and center tube of the pan before turning out the cake onto a rack. Serve warm.

10 to 12 servings

a buttery nursery rhyme

Come, butter, come
Come, butter, come;
Peter stands at the gate
Waiting for a butter cake,
Come, butter, come.

This old English nursery rhyme made it across the Atlantic and was heard chanted by a butter maker as she churned as recently as 1936 in southern Indiana, according to the *Oxford Dictionary of Nursery Rhymes* (1951). Marjorie Kinnan Rawlings reported a similar version of the rhyme in Florida in her book *Cross Creek Cookery* (1942).

Lindy's New York Cheesecake

Cheesecakes are old, known to the ancient Greeks and popular over the centuries throughout Europe. The quintessential American cheesecake, a sweet, creamy, sinfully rich cake, was developed at Lindy's in New York, a restaurant known more for its clientele of celebrities than for its food. According to legend, waiters at Lindy's can be bribed to reveal the "secret" recipe. No doubt the bribery has been widespread because this version is quite well known.

Cookie Dough Crust

1 cup unbleached all-purpose flour

3 tablespoons sugar

1 teaspoon finely grated lemon zest

⅛ teaspoon salt

½ cup (1 stick) butter, cut into ¼-inch cubes

1 large egg yolk

½ teaspoon pure vanilla extract

1. First make the crust. Combine the flour, sugar, lemon zest, and salt in a large bowl or food processor. With a pastry blender, with your fingertips, or with the food processor, cut or rub the butter into the flour mixture until it has the consistency of coarse crumbs. Add the egg yolk and vanilla. Mix until combined. Wrap in plastic and refrigerate for 45 minutes.

2. Preheat the oven to 400°F. Pat out the dough over the bottom and 2 inches up the sides of a 9-inch springform pan.

3. Bake the crust for 10 minutes. Remove the pan from the oven and set aside to cool. Reduce the oven temperature to 325°F.

Cheese Filling

2½ pounds cream cheese (five 8-ounce packages), at room temperature

1¾ cups sugar

3 tablespoons unbleached all-purpose flour

2 teaspoons finely grated lemon zest

1 teaspoon freshly squeezed lemon juice

1 teaspoon pure vanilla extract

5 large eggs

2 large egg yolks

¼ cup heavy whipping cream

4. To make the cheese filling, beat the batter by hand. If you use an electric mixer, avoid beating on very high speed because this incorporates too much air into the cheesecake and causes it to rise (and fall) like a soufflé. Use a large mixing bowl and beat the cream cheese until it is creamy and smooth. Combine the sugar and flour and beat into the cream cheese. Add the lemon zest, lemon juice, and vanilla. Beat in the eggs and egg yolks, one at a time. Mix well after each addition. Beat in the cream, mixing until smooth. Pour the cheese mixture into the crust-lined pan and smooth the surface.

5. Bake the cake for 1 hour to 1 hour 15 minutes, until the center appears set but not firm.

6. Set the cake in a draft-free place until completely cooled; the cake will become firm as it cools.

7. Gently run a sharp knife around the edge of pan. Refrigerate until thoroughly chilled. Remove the sides of the pan and serve.

NOTE: The original Lindy's recipe used a cookie dough crust, but if you prefer a crumb crust, prepare a graham cracker crust instead. Lightly grease a 9-inch springform pan. Preheat the oven to 325°F. Combine 1½ cups finely ground graham cracker crumbs, 3 tablespoons sugar, 6 tablespoons melted butter, and ¼ teaspoon cinnamon. Press firmly into the bottom and 2 inches up the sides of the pan. Bake for 5 minutes. Set aside on a rack to cool.

8 to 10 servings

Baked Alaska

This dessert dates back to American scientist Benjamin Thompson, later awarded the name Count Rumford for his studies of the resistance of stiffly beaten egg whites to heat. Rumford's "omelette surprise" eventually became the baked Alaska we know today, a brick of ice cream atop a cake layer, covered in meringue. The recipe gets high marks for its actual simplicity, despite the appearance of difficulty.

9-inch round sponge cake (see Note, below)

1 quart chocolate ice cream

1 quart coffee ice cream

6 large egg whites, at room temperature

½ teaspoon cream of tartar

Pinch of salt

¾ cup sugar

1 teaspoon vanilla extract

Warm Chocolate Sauce (recipe follows) (optional)

1. The cake should be about 1 inch tall. If it is any taller, cut it horizontally to make a 1-inch layer. Save the leftover cake for another use. Place the 1-inch cake layer on an aluminum foil-covered board or on a flameproof serving platter.

2. Let the chocolate ice cream stand at room temperature until it is soft enough to mold, but do not allow it to melt. Spread a layer of the ice cream on the cake, leaving a bare border of about 1 inch all the way around the outer edge of the cake. Freeze until firm.

3. Let the coffee ice cream stand at room temperature until it is soft enough to mold, but do not allow it to melt. Mound the coffee ice cream on top of the chocolate layer. Freeze until firm.

4. Cover the cake and ice cream with plastic wrap and freeze thoroughly.

5. Preheat the oven to 475°F with a rack in the lower third of the oven.

6. To make the meringue, beat the egg whites with an electric mixer until foamy. Add the cream of tartar and salt and beat until soft peaks form. Gradually add the sugar, 2 tablespoons at a time, beating until the egg whites are stiff but not dry. The egg whites should hold their shape and remain moist. Beat in the vanilla.

7. Remove the cake and ice cream from the freezer. Peel off the plastic wrap. Quickly spread the meringue over the ice cream and cake, making certain that the cake and ice cream are completely covered. Seal the meringue to the serving board or platter. (If desired, the dessert can be returned to the freezer at this point, for up to 2 hours.)

8. Bake the dessert for 3 to 5 minutes, until the meringue is lightly browned.

9. Serve immediately, passing the warm chocolate sauce on the side.

NOTES:

• You can use a purchased sponge cake or the thin sponge cake used for the Jelly Roll on page 80, adapted as described in the Note there.

• The egg whites in this recipe are not completely cooked. Please see "Egg Information" on page 198.

10 to 12 servings

Warm Chocolate Sauce

8 ounces semisweet chocolate, chopped

1 cup heavy whipping cream

½ teaspoon powdered instant coffee or powdered espresso (optional)

1. In a heavy saucepan over low heat or in a double boiler set over simmering water, combine the chocolate, cream, and instant coffee (if using). Stir until the chocolate is melted and the sauce is smooth.

2. Remove from the heat and serve at once, or hold in the refrigerator for up to 1 week and reheat before serving. If the sauce is too stiff, stir in a little milk or brewed coffee to thin it.

About 1½ cups

Lemon Pudding Cake

As the title suggests, this lovely, lemony dessert is a cross between a pudding and a cake. To gild this lily, serve with cream, fresh berries, or a raspberry sauce made by puréeing a 10-ounce package of sweetened frozen berries.

1 cup sugar

¼ cup unbleached all-purpose flour

⅛ teaspoon salt

2 tablespoons butter, melted

1 tablespoon finely grated lemon zest

5 tablespoons freshly squeezed lemon juice (about 2 medium-sized lemons)

3 large egg yolks

1½ cups milk

3 egg whites, at room temperature

⅛ teaspoon cream of tartar

1. Preheat the oven to 350°F. Lightly grease a 1½-quart baking dish or 6 custard cups. Set into a slightly larger pan that is at least 2 inches deep.

2. In a mixing bowl, combine ¾ cup of the sugar, the flour, and salt. Add the butter, lemon zest, and lemon juice. Mix until thoroughly blended.

3. With a whisk, beat the egg yolks until thick and lemon colored. Add the milk and mix well. Combine with the lemon mixture, stirring until blended.

4. In another bowl, beat the egg whites until foamy. Add the cream of tartar and beat until soft peaks form. Add the remaining ¼ cup of sugar gradually, and beat until the egg whites are stiff but not dry. The egg whites should hold their shape and remain moist. Fold the whites into the lemon mixture. Spoon into the baking dish or custard cups. Pour 1 inch of hot water into the larger pan, surrounding the baking dish or custard cups with hot water.

5. Bake in the baking dish for 45 minutes or in the custard cups for 35 minutes, or until the pudding is set and the top is golden brown.

6. Remove the baking dish or custard cups from the water bath and let cool on a rack. Serve warm or chilled.

6 servings

frosted to perfection

Even a perfectly baked cake may suffer a tarnished reputation if its frosting isn't up to par. Making the frosting is only half the battle; many would say that correctly applying the frosting is more difficult.

The techniques below explain how to frost a layer cake, a challenging cake to frost; modify these techniques for other types of cakes. After all, it's only fair that your cake look as good as it tastes!

1. Start with a completely cooled cake. Brush off any crumbs and, if necessary, cut away any crisp edges.

2. Most frostings work best if made just before they are spread. Creamy, uncooked frostings can be held in the refrigerator for a few hours if they are kept tightly covered. Warm to room temperature and stir well before using.

3. To keep the cake plate clean, place strips of waxed paper around the edges of the plate. These can be removed later.

4. Place the first layer top-side down on the cake plate. Using a frosting spatula, spread with frosting almost to the edge.

5. Place the second layer, top-side up, on the bottom layer.

6. Spread about three quarters of the remaining frosting on the sides. Hold the frosting spatula so that the tip rests on the cake plate. The straight edge of the blade should be held against the frosting so that the flat side of the blade forms a 30-degree angle with the side of the cake. Spread the frosting evenly on the sides. Don't worry about the ridge of frosting that piles up on the top of the cake. You will use that to cover the top.

7. With your spatula held horizontally and level, spread the remaining frosting on top of the cake, working from the edge to the center.

8. Use the back of a spoon to swirl circles and wavy lines in the frosting; pull up for peaks.

Chocolate Frosting

3 ounces unsweetened chocolate

3 tablespoons butter

3 cups sifted confectioners' sugar

Pinch of salt

7 tablespoons milk, at room temperature

1 teaspoon pure vanilla extract

1. Combine the chocolate and butter in a medium-sized saucepan. Melt over very low heat, stirring until combined.

2. Blend in the confectioners' sugar and salt alternately with the milk and vanilla, mixing until the frosting is smooth and has a good consistency for spreading.

Frosting for two 8- or 9-inch layers or a 9- by 13-inch cake

RECOMMENDED ON:

Chocolate Layer Cake, page 50

Banana Cake, page 55

Carrot Cake, page 70

Gold Cake, page 82

Glossy Chocolate Glaze

1 cup (6 ounces) semisweet chocolate chips or chopped dark sweet baking chocolate

4 tablespoons butter

1 tablespoon light corn syrup

1. In a heavy-bottomed saucepan, combine the chocolate, butter, and corn syrup. Cook over low heat, stirring until the mixture is melted and smooth.

2. Cool for about 10 minutes, stirring occasionally. Then spread or pour over the cake.

Glaze for the top and sides of an 8- or 9-inch layer cake

RECOMMENDED ON:

Chocolate Layer Cake, page 50

Angel Food Cake, page 76

Sponge Cake, page 78

Gold Cake, page 82

Vanilla Frosting

4 tablespoons butter, at room
temperature

2 teaspoons finely grated lemon zest

3 cups sifted confectioners' sugar

2 to 3 tablespoons cream or milk

1 teaspoon pure vanilla extract

RECOMMENDED ON:

Chocolate Layer Cake,
page 50

Banana Cake, page 55

1. Beat the butter with the lemon zest until creamy. Gradually add half of the confectioners' sugar, blending thoroughly.

2. Beat in 2 tablespoons of the cream, the vanilla, and the remaining 1½ cups of confectioners' sugar. Add enough cream to make a smooth frosting of spreading consistency.

Frosting for two 8- or 9-inch layers or a 9- by 13-inch cake

Seven-Minute Frosting

2 large egg whites

1½ cups sugar

⅓ cup water

¼ teaspoon cream of tartar

Pinch of salt

1 teaspoon pure vanilla extract

RECOMMENDED ON:

Lady Baltimore Cake,
page 56

Spice Cake, page 58

Black Walnut Cake,
page 73

1. In the top of a double boiler, combine the egg whites, sugar, water, cream of tartar, and salt. Place over simmering water (upper pan should not touch water) and beat with an electric hand mixer or rotary beater for 7 minutes, or until stiff peaks form.

2. Remove the pan from the boiling water, add the vanilla, and beat for another minute on high speed.

Frosting for two 8- or 9-inch layers or a 9- by 13-inch cake

Burnt Sugar Icing

¼ cup granulated sugar

⅓ cup boiling water

3 tablespoons butter, at room temperature

2¼ cups sifted confectioners' sugar

1 teaspoon pure vanilla extract

RECOMMENDED ON:

Pound Cake, page 51

Spice Cake, page 58

Black Walnut Cake, page 73

1. In a small heavy saucepan or skillet, cook the granulated sugar over medium heat, without stirring, until the sugar melts and the syrup becomes a deep golden brown, about 5 minutes.

2. Remove from the heat. Slowly and carefully pour in the boiling water. (The water will steam and boil up as it hits the caramelized sugar.) Return the pan to a low heat and stir the mixture until the sugar is completely dissolved. Cool.

3. In a medium-sized bowl, beat the butter until creamy. Gradually add half the confectioners' sugar, blending well. The mixture will be lumpy. Beat in 3 tablespoons of the cooled burnt sugar syrup and the vanilla. Blend in the remaining confectioners' sugar and additional syrup to make a smooth frosting of spreading consistency.

Frosting for two 8- or 9-inch layers or a 9- by 13-inch cake

Cream Cheese Frosting

½ cup (1 stick) butter, at room temperature

1 package (8 ounces) cream cheese, at room temperature

2 teaspoons finely grated orange zest

2 cups sifted confectioners' sugar

RECOMMENDED ON:

German Chocolate Cake, page 48

Chocolate Layer Cake, page 50

Spice Cake, page 58

Carrot Cake, page 70

In a bowl, beat the butter and cream cheese until creamy and well blended. Beat in the orange zest. Gradually add the confectioners' sugar, beating until smooth.

Frosting for two 8- or 9-inch layers or a 9- by 13-inch cake

Orange Frosting

RECOMMENDED ON:

Sponge Cake, page 78

Gold Cake, page 82

4 tablespoons butter, at room temperature	3 cups sifted confectioners' sugar
1 tablespoon finely grated orange zest	About ¼ cup freshly squeezed orange juice

1. Beat the butter with the orange zest until creamy. Gradually add half the confectioners' sugar, blending thoroughly.

2. Beat in 2 tablespoons of the orange juice; then add the remaining 1½ cups of confectioners' sugar. Add enough orange juice to make a creamy frosting of spreading consistency.

Frosting for two 8- or 9-inch layers or a 9- by 13-inch cake

Coconut Pecan Frosting

RECOMMENDED ON:

German Chocolate Cake, page 48

Spice Cake, page 58

3 large egg yolks	1 teaspoon pure vanilla extract
1 cup evaporated milk (from a 12-ounce can)	1 cup chopped pecans
¾ cup firmly packed light brown sugar	1¼ cups lightly packed, flaked sweetened coconut
½ cup (1 stick) butter	

1. In a heavy-bottomed saucepan, beat the egg yolks lightly with a wire whisk. Add the evaporated milk, brown sugar, and butter. Cook over low heat, stirring, until the mixture thickens, 8 to 10 minutes. Do not boil.

2. Remove the saucepan from the heat. Stir in the vanilla. Cool, stirring frequently.

3. Add the pecans and coconut and beat until the frosting is of spreading consistency.

Frosting for two 8- or 9-inch layers or a 9- by 13-inch cake

Sea Foam Frosting

2 large egg whites
1½ cups firmly packed light brown sugar
⅓ cup water

¼ teaspoon cream of tartar
Pinch of salt
1 teaspoon pure vanilla extract

RECOMMENDED ON:
Banana Cake, page 55
Spice Cake, page 58
Black Walnut Cake,
page 73

1. In the top of a double boiler, combine the egg whites, brown sugar, water, cream of tartar, and salt. Place over simmering water (the water should not touch the bottom of the pan) and beat with an electric hand mixer or rotary beater for 7 minutes, or until the mixture forms stiff peaks.

2. Remove the pan from the boiling water, add the vanilla, and beat for another minute on high speed, until the frosting is thick enough to spread.

Frosting for two 8- or 9-inch layers or a 9- by 13-inch cake

Brown Sugar Frosting

1½ cups firmly packed dark brown sugar
5 tablespoons cream
1 tablespoon butter

Pinch of salt
½ teaspoon pure vanilla extract

RECOMMENDED ON:
Applesauce Cake,
page 66
Poppy Seed Cake,
page 74

1. In a small saucepan, combine the brown sugar, cream, butter, and salt. Cook over medium heat, stirring constantly, until the mixture comes to a boil.

2. Remove from the heat. Cool slightly, then add the vanilla and beat until the frosting is cool and slightly thickened. If the frosting gets too thick, add a few drops of cream.

Frosting for a 9-inch square or tube cake

3 • Pies

Apple Pie

Apples and apple pie were both well known in the Old World. Indeed, there are indications that apples were known to the people of the Iron Age and were cultivated in Egypt some 4,000 years ago. The Pilgrims brought with them apple seeds and lost no time in getting trees established. Apple orchards were so valuable that by 1648 Governor John Endicott was able to trade 500 apple trees for 250 acres of land. By the end of the nineteenth century, some 8,000 apple varieties were listed with the U.S. Department of Agriculture. Is it any wonder that apple pie became one of America's most popular desserts?

Pastry for a 9-inch double-crust pie (see page 146)

¾ cup plus 1 tablespoon sugar, or more to taste

2 tablespoons unbleached all-purpose flour

1½ teaspoons ground cinnamon

¼ teaspoon ground allspice

¼ teaspoon freshly grated nutmeg

3½ to 4 pounds tart, crisp apples, peeled, cored, sliced ¼ inch thick (8 cups)

1 teaspoon finely grated lemon zest

1 tablespoon freshly squeezed lemon juice

2 tablespoons butter, cut into small pieces

1 teaspoon milk

Cheddar cheese or vanilla ice cream, to serve

1. Prepare the pie dough according to the recipe directions and refrigerate.

2. In a large bowl, combine ¾ cup of the sugar, the flour, cinnamon, allspice, and nutmeg. Add the apples; sprinkle with the lemon zest and lemon juice. Toss together to mix thoroughly. If the apples are too tart, add a little extra sugar.

3. Preheat the oven to 425°F with a rack in the lower third of the oven.

4. To prepare the pie shell, lightly flour a work surface. Roll out the larger portion of the chilled dough to a thickness of about ⅛ inch. Fit into a 9-inch pie plate, leaving a 1-inch overhang. Spoon the apple mixture into the pastry, mounding it higher in the center. Dot with butter. Roll out the remaining dough into a circle about 1 inch larger than the pie plate. Moisten the

edge of the bottom crust with water. Fold the dough circle in half, lift off the work surface, place the pastry across the center of the filled pie, and unfold. Trim the edge ½ inch larger than the pie plate and tuck the overhang under the edge of the bottom crust. Crimp the edges with a fork or make a fluted pattern with your fingers. Make several decorative slits in the top crust to allow steam to escape. Place the pie on a baking sheet to catch any juices that overflow.

5. Bake the pie in the lower third of the oven for 20 minutes. Reduce the heat to 350°F and continue to bake for 30 minutes. Brush the top of the pie with the milk and sprinkle with the remaining 1 tablespoon of sugar. Bake for 10 to 15 minutes longer, until the crust is golden and the juices are bubbly.

6. Cool the pie on a rack. Serve warm or at room temperature with slices of Cheddar cheese or vanilla ice cream.

6 to 8 servings

But, I, when I undress me
Each night, upon my knees
Will ask the Lord to bless me
With apple-pie and cheese.

— Eugene Field, "Apple-Pie and Cheese"

Crumb-Topped Sour Cream Apple Pie

If an old-fashioned dessert is as rich as it can possibly be, chances are it was developed by the Pennsylvania Dutch, who were not Dutch at all. They were German-speaking religious refugees who settled in Pennsylvania. Although these settlers followed a fairly austere lifestyle, their tables were generously laden with foods of all kinds. Some food historians are convinced that the Pennsylvania Dutch are responsible for the development of American fruit pies (though other historians think fruit pies are of New England origin). This apple pie, with its rich filling enhanced with sour cream and its crumb topping, is Pennsylvania Dutch in origin.

Pie Shell and Filling

Pastry for a 9-inch single-crust pie (see page 146)

2 tablespoons unbleached all-purpose flour

½ cup granulated sugar, or more to taste

¼ teaspoon freshly grated nutmeg

⅛ teaspoon salt

1 large egg

1 cup sour cream

1 teaspoon pure vanilla extract

6 large tart, crisp apples, peeled, cored, and sliced ⅛ inch thick

Crumb Topping

½ cup unbleached all-purpose flour

⅓ cup firmly packed dark brown sugar

1 teaspoon ground cinnamon

⅛ teaspoon salt

4 tablespoons butter, at room temperature

½ cup chopped walnuts (optional)

1. Prepare the pie shell according to the recipe directions and refrigerate.

2. Preheat the oven to 400°F with a rack in the lower third of the oven.

3. In a large bowl, combine the flour, granulated sugar, nutmeg, and salt. Add the egg, sour cream, and vanilla and whisk until smooth. Add the apples and toss until the apples are well coated. If the apples are too tart, add a little extra sugar.

4. Spoon the apple mixture into the pie shell. Place the pie on a baking sheet to catch any juices that overflow.

5. Bake in the lower third of the oven for 15 minutes. Reduce the heat to 350°F and cover the pie loosely with aluminum foil (do not let the foil touch the apples). Continue to bake for about 40 minutes, until an apple pierced with a knife is tender.

6. While the pie bakes, prepare the crumb topping. Combine the flour, brown sugar, cinnamon, and salt. With your fingers, rub in the butter until it resembles coarse crumbs. Mix in the walnuts (if using).

7. Remove the foil from the pie. Sprinkle the topping over the pie. Bake for 10 to 15 minutes, until the topping is golden.

8. Cool the pie on a rack before serving warm or at room temperature.

Serves 6 to 8

The friendly cow all red and white,
I love with all my heart:
She gives me cream with all her might,
To eat with apple tart.

— Robert Louis Stevenson, "The Cow"

Blueberry Pie

Eat in any diner in New England during the summer and you are likely to find blueberry pie on the menu. If you are lucky, the pie will be filled with fresh berries. Unlucky travelers will be served a sweet, blue, gluey concoction that goes by the name of blueberry pie. In that case, it's best to bake your own.

Pastry for a 9-inch double-crust pie
(see page 146)

6 cups fresh blueberries

¾ cup sugar

5 tablespoons unbleached all-purpose flour

1 teaspoon ground cinnamon

¼ teaspoon freshly grated nutmeg

Pinch of salt

1 tablespoon freshly squeezed lemon juice

1 tablespoon butter, cut into pieces

1 large egg, beaten

1 tablespoon water

1. Prepare the pie dough according to the recipe directions and refrigerate.

2. Rinse and sort the blueberries. Drain thoroughly on paper towels.

3. In a large bowl, combine the sugar, flour, cinnamon, nutmeg, and salt. Add the blueberries. Sprinkle with the lemon juice. Toss lightly to combine. Set aside.

4. Preheat the oven to 425°F with a rack in the lower third of the oven.

5. To prepare the pie shell, lightly flour a work surface. Roll out the larger portion of the refrigerated dough to a thickness of about ⅛ inch. Fit into a 9-inch pie plate, leaving a 1-inch overhang. Spoon the filling into the pastry. Dot with butter. Roll out the remaining dough into a circle about 1 inch larger than the pie plate. Moisten the edge of the bottom crust with water. Fold the dough circle in half, lift off the work surface, place it across the center of the filled pie, and unfold. Trim the edge ½ inch larger than the pie plate and tuck the overhang under the edge of the bottom crust. Crimp the edges with a fork or make a fluted pattern with your fingers. Make several decorative slits in the top crust to allow steam to escape.

6. Make an egg wash by combining the egg with the water. Brush the top of the pie with the egg wash. Place the pie on a baking sheet to catch any juices that overflow.

7. Bake in the lower third of the oven for 15 minutes. Reduce the oven temperature to 350°F and bake for 40 to 45 minutes longer, until the crust is golden brown.

8. Cool the pie on a rack. Serve warm or at room temperature.

6 to 8 servings

maine blueberry festival

The annual state of Maine Wild Blueberry Festival is held during the last week in August in Union, Maine. Here's your chance to eat free blueberry pies, which are baked on the fairgrounds and served to everyone who stops in at the Blueberry Hut each afternoon. You can begin each day with blueberry pancakes, meet the reigning blueberry princess, and spend your mornings sampling fresh blueberries, blueberry jam, and blueberry syrup. Don't forget the blueberry pie–eating contest.

For more information, contact the Maine Wild Blueberry Festival (see Resources, page 198).

Lattice-Top Sour Cherry Pie

It takes a dedicated baker to make a sour cherry pie from scratch. First you must stake out your tree and harvest the fruits before the birds get them. Then you must pit the cherries, a laborious process that is unrewarding unless done in the company of kids who enjoy seeing how far a pit can fly when properly popped out of a cherry. A gadget exists for stoning cherries, but a paper clip works just as well. If this kind of labor isn't fun, rely on canned cherries.

Pastry for a 9-inch double-crust pie (see page 146)

2 cans (16 ounces each) water-packed pitted sour cherries or 6 to 7 cups pitted fresh sour cherries

¾ cup plus 1 tablespoon sugar

3 tablespoons cornstarch

Pinch of salt

1 teaspoon freshly squeezed lemon juice

¼ teaspoon almond extract

⅛ teaspoon ground cloves

1 tablespoon butter, cut into small pieces

1 teaspoon milk

1. Prepare the pie dough according to the recipe directions and refrigerate.

2. If you are using canned cherries, drain the cherries and reserve ⅓ cup of the juice. If you are using fresh cherries, combine the cherries with 3 tablespoons of water in a large saucepan. Heat the mixture to boiling, stirring gently for 1 minute. Remove the saucepan from the heat and drain off the juice to measure ⅓ cup. If there isn't enough liquid, add more water. Cool the juice completely.

3. In a heavy saucepan, combine ¾ cup of the sugar, the cornstarch, and salt. Add the cherry juice and stir with a whisk until blended. Cook over medium heat, stirring until the sugar is dissolved. Boil for 2 to 3 minutes, stirring constantly until the mixture is slightly thickened. Remove from heat; stir in the lemon juice, almond extract, and cloves. Carefully mix in the cherries. Set aside to cool.

4. Preheat the oven to 425°F with a rack in the lower third of the oven.

5. To prepare the pie shell, roll out the larger portion of the refrigerated dough to a thickness of about ⅛ inch. Fit into a 9-inch pie plate, leaving a 1-inch overhang. Spoon the cooled filling into the pastry. Dot with butter. Roll out the remaining dough into a rectangle about ⅛ inch thick and 11 inches long. Trim the ragged edges. Using a pastry wheel or sharp knife, cut the rectangle into 10 lengthwise strips, each ½ inch wide. To form the lattice, lay five strips across the filling, each 1 inch apart. Working from the center, interweave the remaining strips, one at a time, over and under the first strips. Trim the ends. Moisten the overhanging edge of the bottom crust and fold up over ends of the strips. Flute the edge of the crust. Brush the lattice strips with milk; sprinkle with the remaining 1 tablespoon of sugar. Place the pie on a baking sheet to catch any juices that overflow.

6. Bake in the lower third of the oven for 15 minutes. Reduce the oven temperature to 350°F and bake for an additional 30 minutes, or until the crust is golden brown and the juices are bubbly.

7. Cool the pie on a wire rack. Serve warm or at room temperature.

6 to 8 servings

To make a light, crisp, and flaky crust, use a good, fine flour and none but the best butter. Have everything, including yourself, cool. A marble slab makes the best pastry-board. Use a glass rolling-pin, if convenient; if not, one made from hard wood with movable handles. Always use ice or very cold water in mixing, and keep the paste in a cold place. . . . No matter how light your paste may be, the substance of each stratum is dense and hard of digestion, and should never be eaten by persons of weak digestive powers.

– Mrs. Rorer's Cook Book, A Manual of Home Economics by Mrs. S. T. Rorer
(Philadelphia: Arnold and Company, 1866)

Shaker Lemon Pie

"Shaker" is the popular name for members of the United Society of Believers in Christ's Second Appearing. The Shakers originated in England in 1774. They were called Shaking Quakers because of the trembling the believers experienced as a result of their religious emotions. Shakers practiced celibacy and lived communally. They grew strong in America under the leadership of Ann Lee, and 18 Shaker communities were founded by 1826. These communities no longer exist, but the Shakers left behind a legacy of fine furniture designs, handicrafts, and recipes. Interestingly, this lemon pie is said to have been particularly beloved by Shakers because it was made with the one fruit they themselves did not grow.

2 large lemons

2 cups sugar

Pastry for a 9-inch double-crust pie (see page 146)

4 large eggs, lightly beaten

Pinch of salt

1. Slice the lemons paper thin. Remove any seeds. Combine the lemon slices and sugar in a medium-sized bowl and toss to mix. Cover and let stand for at least 8 hours, or overnight. Toss occasionally to disperse the sugar.

2. Prepare the pie dough according to the recipe directions and refrigerate.

3. Preheat the oven to 450°F.

4. Add the eggs and salt to the lemon mixture. Mix well. Set aside.

5. To prepare the pie shell, lightly flour a work surface. Roll out the larger portion of the refrigerated dough to a thickness of about ⅛ inch. Fit into a 9-inch pie plate, leaving a 1-inch overhang. Spoon the filling into the pastry. Roll out the remaining dough into a circle about 1 inch larger than the pie plate. Moisten the edge of the bottom crust with water. Fold the dough circle in half, lift off the board, place the pastry across the center of the filled pie, and unfold.

Trim the edge ½ inch larger than the pie plate and tuck the overhang under the edge of the bottom crust. Crimp the edges with a fork or make a fluted pattern with your fingers. Make several decorative slits in the top crust to allow steam to escape.

6. Bake for 15 minutes. Reduce the oven temperature to 350°F and bake for an additional 20 to 25 minutes, until a knife inserted near the edge of the pie comes out clean. If the top of the crust begins to brown too deeply, cover loosely with foil.

7. Cool the pie on a wire rack before serving warm or at room temperature.

6 to 8 servings

rolling pins

Rolling pins were not always the cylindrical affairs they are today. In Southern plantation kitchens of the 1700s, the rolling pin had a large U-shaped handle that could be grasped in the middle and operated with one hand. This left the other hand free to work the dough — an improvement on the rolling pin design of today.

Strawberry-Rhubarb Pie

Pie plant, as rhubarb is also known, is native to Asia and eastern Europe, where it is valued both for medicinal properties and for eating. You can't do much with rhubarb but cook it with plenty of sugar or honey to make a sauce or a pie. Conveniently, the tart rhubarb matures just as sweet strawberries ripen, allowing for a marriage that was surely arranged in heaven.

Pastry for a 9-inch double-crust pie (see page 146)

1¼ cups plus 1 tablespoon sugar

⅓ cup unbleached all-purpose flour

1 teaspoon finely grated orange zest

Pinch of salt

1 pound fresh rhubarb, cut into 1-inch pieces (4 cups)

2 cups halved strawberries

2 tablespoons butter

1 teaspoon milk

Whipped cream or vanilla yogurt, to serve

1. Prepare the pie dough according to the recipe directions and refrigerate.

2. In a large bowl, combine 1¼ cup of the sugar, the flour, orange zest, and salt. Add the rhubarb and strawberries and toss lightly to combine. Set aside.

3. Preheat the oven to 425°F with a rack in the lower third of the oven.

4. To prepare the pie shell, lightly flour a work surface. Roll out the larger portion of the refrigerated dough to a thickness of about ⅛ inch. Fit into a 9-inch pie plate, leaving a 1-inch overhang. Spoon the filling into the pastry. Dot with butter. Roll out the remaining dough into a rectangle about ⅛ inch thick and 11 inches long. Trim the ragged edges. Using a pastry wheel or sharp knife, cut the rectangle into 10 lengthwise strips, each ½ inch wide. To form the lattice, lay five strips across the filling, each 1 inch apart. Working from the center, interweave the remaining strips, one at a time, over and under the first strips. Trim the ends. Moisten the overhanging edge of the bottom crust and fold up over the ends of the strips. Flute the edge of the crust. Brush the lattice strips with milk; sprinkle with the remaining 1 tablespoon of sugar. Place the pie on a baking sheet to catch any juices that overflow.

5. Bake in the lower third of the oven for 15 minutes. Reduce the oven temperature to 350°F and bake for an additional 50 minutes, or until the filling is bubbly and the crust is golden brown.

6. Cool the pie on a wire rack. Serve warm or at room temperature topped with whipped cream or vanilla yogurt.

6 to 8 servings

pie mania

By a certain definition, a Yankee is one who eats pie for breakfast. But the early great pie makers were probably from Dixie. According to food historians, pie making became something of a mania in the South in the nineteenth century. This coincided with the drop in the price of white sugar as the cane sugar industry developed in the States. No more did cooks have to depend on strongly flavored honey and sorghum to sweeten their pastries. Instead, they could whip up such blandly sweet delights as Chess Pie, Pecan Pie, and Lemon Meringue Pie.

Deep-Dish Peach Pie

One has to live in peach country — the Southeast, New Jersey, or the Pacific Northwest — to enjoy a perfect tree-ripened peach these days. For the rest of us, peaches bought a few days in advance and left to ripen in a paper bag with a banana or an apple will do. (The banana or apple produces a gas that hastens ripening.)

Cream Cheese Pastry (page 149)

6 cups fresh peeled, sliced peaches

¼ cup firmly packed light brown sugar, or to taste

3 tablespoons unbleached all-purpose flour

⅛ teaspoon freshly grated nutmeg

2 tablespoons butter, cut into small pieces

1 large egg yolk

2 teaspoons water

1 teaspoon granulated sugar

Vanilla ice cream or whipped cream, to serve

1. Prepare the pastry dough according to the recipe directions and refrigerate.

2. Preheat the oven to 375°F. Place the peaches in an 8-inch square baking dish or 2-quart casserole.

3. In a small bowl, combine the brown sugar, flour, and nutmeg. Toss with the peaches, mixing gently until they are thoroughly coated. If the peaches lack flavor, add a little more brown sugar. Dot with the butter.

4. On a lightly floured work surface, roll out the pastry into a square or circle 1 inch larger than the baking dish. Roll the pastry onto the rolling pin and then gently drape it over the top of the dish. Crimp the edges of the pastry and press around the top of the dish.

5. Brush the top crust with an egg wash made by beating the egg yolk with the water. Sprinkle with the granulated sugar. With the tip of a sharp knife, cut three or four slits in the top of the pastry to allow steam to escape.

6. Bake for 35 to 40 minutes, until the crust is golden.

7. Serve warm along with vanilla ice cream or whipped cream.

6 servings

Chess Pie

How did this Southern specialty get its name? A few stories circulate, none of which has anything to do with the ancient board game. Some claim that a chess pie was originally a "chest pie" that would keep in a cupboard without refrigeration. Some say that it is an adaptation of the English cheese pie. Then there is the story of the plantation cook who was asked what she was making. "Jes' pie," she replied. Whatever the origin, today there are many variations. One variation — called a Jefferson Davis Pie — contains spices and dates. This recipe is similar to the Thomas Jefferson Pie.

Pastry for a 9-inch single crust pie (see page 146)

½ cup firmly packed brown sugar

½ cup granulated sugar

6 tablespoons butter, at room temperature

3 large eggs

1 cup chopped pecans

¼ cup heavy whipping cream

1 tablespoon yellow cornmeal

1 tablespoon unbleached all-purpose flour

1½ teaspoons pure vanilla extract

⅛ teaspoon salt

1. Prepare the pie shell according to the recipe directions. Partially bake the shell and let it cool on a rack before filling.

2. Preheat the oven to 350°F.

3. In a large mixing bowl, beat together the brown and granulated sugars and the butter until creamy. Add the eggs, one at a time, beating well after each addition. Stir in the pecans, cream, cornmeal, flour, vanilla, and salt, blending well. Pour the mixture into the pie shell.

4. Bake for 40 to 45 minutes, until a knife inserted 1 inch from the outer edge comes out clean and the filling is slightly firm.

5. Cool on a wire rack. Serve warm or at room temperature, within 3 hours of cooling.

6 to 8 servings

Sour Cream Raisin Pie

We've eaten many different versions of raisin pie in our days. Raisin pies made in Vermont are likely to be sweetened with maple syrup. Some pies are made without sour cream, in which case they bear a striking resemblance to mince pies. This version has a custard base and is delicately spiced.

Pastry for an 8-inch single-crust pie (see page 146)

2 large eggs

¾ cup sugar

1 cup chopped raisins

1 cup sour cream

Zest of 1 lemon, finely grated

1 tablespoon freshly squeezed lemon juice

½ teaspoon ground cinnamon

¼ teaspoon freshly grated nutmeg

Pinch of salt

½ cup chopped walnuts

1. Prepare the pie shell according to the recipe directions. Partially bake the shell (see page 148) and let it cool on a rack before filling.

2. Preheat the oven to 425°F with a rack in the lower third of the oven.

3. In a medium-sized bowl, beat the eggs and sugar with a wire whisk until light and fluffy. Add the raisins, sour cream, lemon zest, lemon juice, cinnamon, nutmeg, and salt, whisking until well blended. Pour the mixture into the pie shell. Sprinkle the walnuts over the top.

4. Bake in the lower third of the oven for 10 minutes. Reduce the oven temperature to 350°F and continue baking for 25 to 30 minutes, until a knife inserted 1 inch from the edge comes out clean. (If the crust browns too quickly, cover the edge with a strip of aluminum foil.)

5. Cool the pie on a rack. Serve at room temperature or refrigerated. Refrigerate any leftover pie.

6 servings

a raisin o' the sun

The summer of 1873 was a hot one, so hot that in California grapes were drying on the vine. It was a financial disaster for the growers — except for one who shipped his dried grapes to a friend in San Francisco who ran a grocery store. The grocer, an enterprising fellow, called the grapes "Peruvian delicacies" simply because there was a Peruvian ship in the harbor at the time and he had no better name for them. The raisins were a sweet success, and grape growing in the San Joaquin Valley was never the same.

But had this grocer known his French, he would have known that the French word for grape is *raisin*. A dried grape is a *raisin sec*. And, in fact, dried grapes or raisins were found in cookery books at least as far back as the 1600s, when they were referred to as "raisins of the sun" by both Shakespeare *(The Winter's Tale)* and cookbook author George Hartman, who wrote *The Closet of the eminently learned Sir Kenelm Digby, kt. opened: whereby is discovered several ways for making of metheglin, sider, cherrywine &c. Together with excellent directions for cookery; as also for preserving, conserving, candying &c.*

Raisins are commonplace today, with California providing nearly half of the world's supply. The most common grapes used for making raisins are Thompson Seedless, Zante, and Muscat. Both dark and golden seedless raisins (sultanas) are made from Thompson Seedless; the difference is that golden raisins have been treated with sulfur dioxide to prevent their color from darkening and are dried with artificial heat to produce moist, plump raisins. Dried currants are actually tiny seedless Zante grapes.

Pumpkin Pie

Pumpkin makes an appearance at most Thanksgiving dinners, often in the form of pie. This classic recipe has just a hint of sophistication from the orange liqueur that rounds out the flavors of spice and pumpkin. Ginger-spiced whipped cream is a wonderful accompaniment.

Pastry for a 9-inch single-crust pie (see page 146)

2 large eggs

¾ cup firmly packed light brown sugar

2 cups cooked or canned puréed pumpkin

1½ cups (12 ounces) evaporated milk

2 tablespoons orange liqueur (Grand Marnier)

1 teaspoon ground cinnamon

1 teaspoon ground ginger

½ teaspoon freshly grated nutmeg

½ teaspoon salt

¼ teaspoon ground allspice

¼ teaspoon ground cloves

Whipped cream or Ginger-Spiced Whipped Cream (recipe follows), for serving

1. Prepare the pie shell according to the recipe directions and refrigerate.

2. Preheat the oven to 425°F with a rack in the lower third of the oven.

3. In a medium-sized bowl, beat together the eggs and brown sugar until light. Add the pumpkin, evaporated milk, orange liqueur, cinnamon, ginger, nutmeg, salt, allspice, and cloves. Mix thoroughly. Pour into the unbaked pie shell.

4. Bake in the lower third of the oven for 15 minutes. Reduce the oven temperature to 325°F and continue baking for 35 to 40 minutes, until the filling is firm and a knife inserted 1 inch from the edge comes out clean.

5. Cool the pie on a wire rack. Serve at room temperature or refrigerated, with whipped cream or Ginger-Spiced Whipped Cream. Refrigerate any leftover pie.

6 to 8 servings

Ginger-Spiced Whipped Cream

1 cup heavy whipping cream

1 tablespoon brandy

2 tablespoons sifted confectioners' sugar

2 tablespoons sour cream

2 tablespoons minced crystallized ginger

1. Beat the cream until soft peaks form. Add the brandy and sugar and beat until stiff.

2. Fold in the sour cream and ginger.

6 to 8 servings

whipped cream

Whipped cream is the perfect topping for many desserts; it should be whipped to perfection, meaning the texture should be light and billowy, not granular.

For perfect whipped cream, start with cold heavy whipping cream, a chilled bowl, and beaters. Start beating slowly, gradually picking up speed. The cream is fully whipped when it forms floppy peaks that droop slightly when spooned. You can hold whipped cream in the refrigerator for about 1 hour.

Sweet Potato Pie

Thought to originate in South America, the sweet potato was cultivated in North America long before Columbus set off from Spain. In the South, sweet potato pies are much more common than pumpkin pies.

Pastry for a 9-inch single-crust pie (see page 146)

2 large eggs

¾ cup firmly packed dark brown sugar

2 cups mashed, cooked sweet potatoes

1½ cups half-and-half or evaporated milk

3 tablespoons butter, melted and cooled

1 tablespoon bourbon or brandy

1 tablespoon unbleached all-purpose flour

1½ teaspoons ground cinnamon

½ teaspoon ground ginger

½ teaspoon freshly grated nutmeg, plus more to serve

½ teaspoon salt

¼ teaspoon ground allspice or mace

¼ teaspoon ground cloves

Whipped cream sweetened with honey, to serve

1. Prepare the pie shell according to the recipe directions and refrigerate.

2. Preheat the oven to 425°F with a rack in the lower third of the oven.

3. In a medium-sized bowl, beat together the eggs and brown sugar until light. Add the sweet potatoes, half-and-half, butter, bourbon, flour, cinnamon, ginger, nutmeg, salt, allspice, and cloves. Mix thoroughly. Pour the mixture into the unbaked pie shell.

4. Bake in the lower third of the oven for 15 minutes. Reduce the oven temperature to 325°F and continue baking for 35 to 40 minutes, until the filling is firm and a knife inserted 1 inch from the edge comes out almost clean. (A little sweet potato will adhere to the knife.)

5. Cool on a rack. Serve at room temperature or refrigerated, with whipped cream sweetened with honey; sprinkle with the freshly grated nutmeg. Refrigerate any leftover pie.

6 to 8 servings

Shoofly Pie

There is some question as to who invented the double-crusted American pie — the Pennsylvania Dutch or New Englanders. But there is no question that shoofly pie came from the Pennsylvania Dutch. This pie, really a molasses sponge cake in a crust, should be tried if only to get a taste of how our ancestors ate. It's awfully sweet, so be prepared to shoo away any flies that are attracted to its sugary aroma.

Pastry for a 9-inch single-crust pie (see page 146)

1¼ cups unbleached all-purpose flour

½ cup firmly packed light brown sugar

½ teaspoon ground cinnamon

¼ teaspoon grated nutmeg

¼ teaspoon salt

4 tablespoons butter, at room temperature

½ teaspoon baking soda

⅔ cup hot water

⅔ cup dark molasses

Light cream, to serve

1. Prepare the pie shell according to the recipe directions and refrigerate.

2. Preheat the oven to 425°F with a rack in the lower third of the oven.

3. In a medium-sized bowl, combine the flour, brown sugar, cinnamon, nutmeg, and salt. Using your fingers, rub the butter into the flour mixture until the mixture has the consistency of coarse meal.

4. Dissolve the baking soda in the hot water; combine with the molasses. Pour one third of the molasses mixture into the unbaked pie shell. Sprinkle with one third of the crumb mixture. Continue layering, ending with the crumb mixture.

5. Bake for 15 minutes. Reduce the oven temperature to 350°F and continue baking for 20 minutes, or until the filling is firm when lightly pressed with your fingertip.

6. Let cool on a wire rack. Serve warm or cold with the light cream.

6 to 8 servings

Pecan Pie

"As American as pecan pie" should be the saying. Pecans, like corn and cranberries, are native to North America and were introduced to the early colonists by the Native Americans. The name is derived from a Native American word meaning "hard-shelled nut."

Thomas Jefferson is often credited with the spread of the pecan's popularity. He planted hundreds of trees at Monticello and gave seedlings to George Washington, who planted them at Mount Vernon, where there are still pecan trees today — most likely descendants of the original planting.

Pastry for a 9-inch single-crust pie (see page 146)

2 tablespoons butter, at room temperature

¾ cup firmly packed dark brown sugar

2 tablespoons unbleached all-purpose flour

¼ teaspoon salt

1 cup light corn syrup

3 large eggs

1 tablespoon dark rum

1 teaspoon pure vanilla extract

1¼ cups toasted pecan halves

Whipped cream flavored with rum or vanilla ice cream, to serve

1. Prepare the pie shell according to the recipe directions. Partially bake the shell (see page 148) and let it cool on a rack before filling.

2. Preheat the oven to 350°F.

3. In a medium-sized bowl, beat the butter until creamy. Add the brown sugar, flour, and salt. Mix until thoroughly combined. Blend in the corn syrup. Add the eggs, one at a time, beating well after each addition. Add the rum and vanilla.

4. Spread the pecans over the piecrust. Pour the egg mixture over the pecans.

5. Bake for 35 to 40 minutes, until the filling is firm.

6. Cool the pie on a wire rack. Serve warm or at room temperature, with whipped cream flavored with rum or with vanilla ice cream.

NOTE: To toast pecans, preheat the oven to 300°F. Place the pecans on a baking sheet and bake them for 6 to 8 minutes, stirring once. Cool.

6 to 8 servings

the pecan: an all-american nut

The pecan, a native American hickory nut (*Carya illinoensis*), is grown mainly in Georgia and Texas, where some 100 million pounds are harvested each year. Rich and buttery in flavor, the pecan is favored for pies and confections and can be substituted in any recipe calling for walnuts. Pecans are, however, much more expensive than walnuts.

Pecans in the shell will keep in an airtight container for 2 to 3 months at room temperature or for up to 6 months in the refrigerator. Shelled nuts will keep for 6 months in the refrigerator or for up to 12 months in the freezer.

Figure that 1 pound of pecans in the shell will yield 2¼ cups of shelled pecans. One pound of shelled pecans equals 3½ to 4 cups.

Buttermilk Pie

When fresh fruits were out of season, buttermilk pie was made, particularly in the South, where biscuits, cakes, and cornbread were frequently made with buttermilk. This pie has outstanding flavor — a cross between cheesecake and custard — with a silken texture.

Buttermilk was a staple of rural America, traditionally made from the sour liquid left after the making of butter. Today buttermilk is usually a thick cultured milk made from nonfat or low-fat milk. It is used to make pancakes and waffles; tender cakes and biscuits; and creamy salad dressings, soups, and sauces. It can be used as a marinade for both Southern fried chicken and tandoori chicken. If you buy a quart for this outstanding pie, you are sure to find plenty of uses for the leftover buttermilk.

Pastry for a 9- or 10-inch single-crust pie (see page 146)

¾ cup sugar

3 tablespoons cornstarch

4 large eggs

1⅔ cups buttermilk

1 cup milk

1 teaspoon pure vanilla extract

¼ teaspoon salt

1. Prepare the pie dough according to the recipe directions. Partially bake the shell (see page 148) and let it cool on a rack before filling.

2. Preheat the oven to 375°F.

3. In a medium-sized mixing bowl, combine the sugar and cornstarch. Whisk until no lumps remain. Add the eggs, buttermilk, milk, vanilla, and salt. Whisk until completely smooth. Pour the filling into the pie shell. (Pour any leftover filling into a ramekin to bake as a custard.)

4. Bake the pie for 40 to 45 minutes, until it is spotted with gold and set, but still slightly wobbly in the center. (Bake individual buttered ramekins for 15 to 20 minutes.) Do not overbake.

5. Let cool on a wire rack. Serve warm or cold.

Serves 6 to 8

Grasshopper Pie

The great American dessert tradition includes many, many convenience recipes, such as super-moist cakes that contain pudding mixes, or tomato soup, or sauerkraut. Then there are recipes developed in food manufacturers' kitchens to expand the use of their products, such as Jell-O sponge cakes and Ritz Cracker mock apple pies. We don't know who conceived the idea of replacing gelatin with marshmallows in this sweet chiffon that was developed in the 1950s, but it works. The filling is a cloud of mellow mint flavor, resting lightly on a crispy chocolate crust. The color of the filling — a bright green — is responsible for the unusual name.

9- or 10-inch Chocolate Crumb Crust (see page 150)

30 large marshmallows (from a 10-ounce package)

½ cup milk

¼ cup crème de menthe

3 tablespoons crème de cacao

1½ cups heavy whipping cream

Chocolate shavings, to garnish

1. Prepare and bake the pie crust according to the recipe directions. Cool completely.

2. In a heavy-bottomed saucepan over moderate heat, combine the marshmallows and milk. Cook, stirring constantly, until the marshmallows have melted, 5 to 7 minutes. Remove from the heat. Cool to room temperature. (Do not refrigerate; the marshmallows will gel.)

3. Add the crème de menthe and crème de cacao, beating thoroughly until combined.

4. Whip the cream until stiff. Fold in the marshmallow mixture. Spoon the filling into the crumb crust. Garnish with the chocolate shavings.

5. Refrigerate the pie for 3 to 4 hours, until firm. The pie will hold for up to 24 hours in the refrigerator.

8 to 10 servings

Black Bottom Pie

This pie is heavenly — a dense chocolate bottom topped by a rum-flavored chiffon. Some black bottom aficionados prefer a gingersnap crust, but we like ours with chocolate.

9- or 10-inch Chocolate Crumb Crust (see page 150)

1 envelope (¼ ounce) unflavored gelatin

¼ cup cold water

4 large eggs, separated

¾ cup sugar

4 teaspoons cornstarch

2 cups hot (not boiling) milk or half-and-half

3 ounces semisweet chocolate, finely chopped, or ½ cup semisweet chocolate chips

2 ounces unsweetened chocolate, finely chopped

1 teaspoon pure vanilla extract

2 tablespoons dark rum

¼ teaspoon cream of tartar

¼ teaspoon salt

1 cup heavy whipping cream

Chocolate shavings, to garnish

1. Prepare and bake the pie crust according to the recipe directions. Cool completely.

2. Sprinkle the gelatin over the water in a small bowl. Stir and set aside to soften.

3. In the top part of a double boiler, make a custard by beating the egg yolks with a wire whisk until thick and lemon colored. Mix in ½ cup of the sugar and the cornstarch. Place over simmering water. Gradually add the hot milk and cook, stirring constantly, until the mixture thickens to heavily coat a metal spoon.

4. Remove the top of the double boiler from the heat. Measure 1 cup of the custard into a small bowl. Add the chopped semisweet and unsweetened chocolates. Beat with a fork until smooth. Add the vanilla and pour into the piecrust. Set aside.

5. To the remaining hot custard mixture, add the softened gelatin, stirring until dissolved. Mix in the rum. Refrigerate or place the pan in a bowl of ice water, stirring until the mixture mounds slightly when dropped from a spoon. It should be cold but not set.

6. Beat the egg whites until foamy. Add the cream of tartar and salt and continue beating until soft peaks form. Gradually add the remaining ¼ cup of sugar and continue beating until the egg whites are stiff but not dry. The egg whites should hold their shape and remain moist. Gently fold into the custard.

7. Whip the cream until stiff. Fold ½ cup of the whipped cream into the custard mixture. Spread the custard over the chocolate layer.

8. Refrigerate the pie for 3 to 4 hours, until firm.

9. Pipe dollops of the remaining whipped cream on top of the pie and sprinkle with the chocolate shavings.

NOTE: The egg whites in this recipe are not cooked. Please see "Egg Information" on page 198.

8 to 10 servings

Who dares deny the truth,
There's poetry in pie?

— Henry Wadsworth Longfellow

Maple Chiffon Pie

Anyone who has ever tasted maple sap knows how much imagination is required to think that such watery fluid could become sweet syrup. So who thought to boil sap into syrup in the first place? Legend has it that an Iroquois chief by the name of Woksis threw a tomahawk into a maple tree before leaving on a hunt. The weather grew warm that day, and sap flowed from the gash in the tree into a container standing below. The squaw who collected the container thought it was filled with plain water and boiled her evening meat in it. The boiling caused the sap to be reduced to syrup, which gave the meat a whole new flavor, and the rest is history.

Pastry for 9-inch single-crust pie
(see page 146)

1 envelope (¼ ounce) unflavored gelatin

¼ cup cold water

3 large eggs, separated

⅔ cup pure maple syrup

⅓ cup hot (not boiling) milk or half-and-half

1 teaspoon pure vanilla extract

⅛ teaspoon cream of tartar

⅛ teaspoon salt

1 cup heavy whipping cream

¼ cup chopped butternuts or walnuts, plus 2 tablespoons finely chopped butternuts or walnuts, to garnish

1. Prepare the pie shell according to the recipe directions. Fully bake the shell (see page 148) and let it cool on a rack before filling.

2. In a small bowl, sprinkle the gelatin over the cold water. Stir and set aside to soften.

3. In the top part of a double boiler, make a custard by beating the egg yolks with a wire whisk until thick and lemon colored. Gradually add the maple syrup and hot milk, mixing until combined. Place the pan over simmering water. Stir constantly until the mixture lightly coats a metal spoon. Add the softened gelatin and stir until the gelatin is dissolved. Add the vanilla.

4. Refrigerate the custard or place the pan in a bowl of ice water, stirring until it mounds slightly when dropped from a spoon. The mixture should be cold but not set.

5. Beat the egg whites until foamy. Add the cream of tartar and salt and beat until the egg whites are stiff but not dry. They should hold their shape and remain moist. Gently fold into the cold custard.

6. Beat the cream until stiff. Fold three quarters of it into the custard, along with ¼ cup of the chopped nuts. Spoon into the piecrust. Refrigerate the pie for 3 to 4 hours, until firm.

7. Just before serving, pipe the remaining whipped cream on top of the pie. Garnish with the remaining 2 tablespoons of chopped nuts.

NOTE: The egg whites in this recipe are not cooked. Please see "Egg Information" on page 198.

6 to 8 servings

maple season

In Vermont, maple sugaring season generally begins in early March, when the days warm up above freezing but the nights stay cold. This is the optimum weather for a good sap run. Throughout the state, there are open hours at sugarhouses and sugar-on-snow parties, where boiling hot syrup is poured on snow to harden into a sticky candy. The Vermont Maple Festival in St. Albans provides an opportunity to learn how maple syrup is made, enjoy some local Vermont and French Canadian music, and consume a lot of maple syrup in the form of maple cotton candy, maple fudge, maple cream, maple sugar candies, doughnuts and fried dough dunked in syrup, and pancakes.

For more information, contact the Vermont Maple Festival Council (see Resources, page 198).

Chocolate Cream Pie

What makes a chocolate cream pie so much more wonderful than the chocolate pudding from which it springs? Undoubtedly, it is the contrasts among the crisp crust, the silken chocolate pudding, and the satiny cream topping. This pie speaks of its old-fashioned country origins, of a time when cream and eggs were plentiful and eaten without a sense of sin.

Pastry for a 9-inch single-crust pie shell (see page 146)

1 cup granulated sugar

¼ cup unbleached all-purpose flour

1 tablespoon cornstarch

¼ teaspoon salt

3 cups milk

2 ounces semisweet chocolate, chopped, or ⅓ cup semisweet chocolate chips

2 ounces unsweetened chocolate, chopped

4 large egg yolks, lightly beaten

1 tablespoon butter, cut into small pieces

1 tablespoon plus 1 teaspoon dark rum

1 teaspoon pure vanilla extract

1 cup whipping heavy cream

1 tablespoon sifted confectioners' sugar

Grated chocolate, to garnish

1. Prepare the pie shell according to the recipe directions. Fully bake the shell (see page 148) and let it cool on a rack before filling.

2. In a heavy saucepan, combine the granulated sugar, flour, cornstarch, and salt. Add the milk gradually, stirring constantly with a wire whisk to remove any lumps. Add the semisweet and unsweetened chocolates. Cook over medium heat, stirring constantly, until the mixture thickens and comes to a boil; continue stirring and boil for 1 minute. Remove from the heat.

3. Gradually stir a few teaspoons of the chocolate mixture into the beaten yolks, mixing constantly until blended. When you have added about ½ cup, pour the yolk mixture back into the pan, stirring until combined. Cook, stirring constantly, for 2 minutes, until thick and smooth. Remove from the heat.

4. Add the butter gradually. Stir in 1 tablespoon of the rum and the vanilla. Pour the filling into the baked crust. Cover the surface of the filling with plastic wrap. Let cool.

5. Refrigerate the pie for 3 to 4 hours, until firm. The pie can be refrigerated for up to 24 hours.

6. Just before serving, whip the cream until soft peaks form. Add the confectioners' sugar and the remaining 1 teaspoon of rum. Beat until stiff. Pipe the whipped cream on top of the pie. Sprinkle with the grated chocolate.

6 to 8 servings

cream pies

Cream pies are associated with the rich bounty of the American Midwest. The first cream pie recipe is probably the one found in *The Improved Housewife*, an 1845 edition by Mrs. A. L. Webster. Her recipe called for five eggs, a pint of sweet, thick cream, sugar, raisins, nutmeg, and a pinch of salt.

Banana Cream Pie

Americans consume more bananas than any other fruit, but too few of them, in our opinion, wind up in this luscious dessert. Incidentally, bananas were cultivated by the Arabs in the seventh century. Eight centuries later, in 1482, Portuguese explorers found the fruit growing on the west coast of Africa and picked up the name Guinea natives used for it — banana.

Pastry for a 9-inch single-crust pie (see page 146)

⅔ cup sugar

3 tablespoons cornstarch

2 tablespoons unbleached all-purpose flour

¼ teaspoon salt

2 cups milk

4 large egg yolks, lightly beaten

2 tablespoons butter, cut into small pieces

1 tablespoon dark rum

1 teaspoon pure vanilla extract

1 cup heavy whipping cream

3 large bananas, sliced

1. Prepare the pie shell according to the recipe directions. Fully bake the shell (see page 148) and let it cool on a rack before filling.

2. In a heavy-bottomed saucepan, make a custard by combining the sugar, cornstarch, flour, and salt. Add the milk gradually, stirring constantly with a wire whisk to remove any lumps. Cook over medium heat, stirring constantly, until the mixture thickens and comes to a boil. Continue stirring and boil for 1 minute. Remove from the heat.

3. Gradually add ½ cup of the custard to the beaten egg yolks, a few teaspoons at a time, mixing constantly until blended. Pour the yolk mixture back into the custard pan, stirring until combined. Cook the custard, stirring constantly, for 2 minutes, until thick and smooth. Remove the pan from the heat.

4. Add the butter gradually to the custard. Stir in the rum and vanilla. Pour the custard into a bowl. Cover the surface with plastic wrap. Cool completely.

5. Whip the cream until stiff. Fold half of the whipped cream into the custard filling.

6. Spoon a thin layer of custard over the bottom of the baked pie shell. Arrange a layer of sliced banana over the filling. Alternate layers of custard and bananas, ending with custard. Pipe the remaining whipped cream on top of the pie.

7. Refrigerate the pie for 3 to 4 hours, until firm.

6 to 8 servings

question:
what food yields the most calories per acre?

Answer: bananas. Within six months of planting, the banana plant is twice as tall as a man. Six months later, the fruit begins to form; in another three or four months, the fruit is ready to be harvested. The plant bears only one bunch of fruit, but that bunch will contain about 90 bananas (some have as many as 140). When the one bunch is cut, the whole plant is chopped down and another one planted. Some varieties can yield 600 to 800 bunches a year per acre — some 9 million calories, which means the banana provides more digestible calories per acre than any other major above-ground crop. Still, bananas aren't the answer to world hunger. To subsist entirely on bananas, a person would have to eat 5 pounds a day.

Coconut Cream Pie

The coconut followed the banana as a tropical fruit that met wide acceptance in America. It is native to Malaysia, though coconuts are now grown in many places around the world. The coconut's global propagation was made possible in part by its ability to float long distances. In fact, coconuts have been known to cross entire oceans!

For many people today, packaged coconut is more convenient to buy and use than fresh. Store unopened canned coconut at room temperature for up to 18 months; coconut in plastic bags, up to six months.

Pastry for a 9-inch single-crust pie (see page 146)

1½ cups lightly packed, sweetened flaked coconut

4 large eggs, separated

⅔ cup plus ½ cup sugar

3 tablespoons cornstarch

2 tablespoons unbleached all-purpose flour

¼ teaspoon plus pinch of salt

2 cups milk

2 tablespoons butter, cut into small pieces

2½ teaspoons pure vanilla extract

1 tablespoon Apricot Glaze (see page 145) or 1 tablespoon melted apple jelly

¼ teaspoon cream of tartar

1. Prepare the pie shell according to the recipe directions. Fully bake the shell (see page 148) and let it cool on a rack before filling.

2. Preheat the oven to 300°F.

3. Spread 1 cup of the coconut on a baking sheet. Toast for 5 to 10 minutes, stirring or shaking the pan occasionally, until the coconut is lightly colored. Set aside.

4. To make the custard, beat the egg yolks lightly in a small bowl. In a heavy-bottomed saucepan, combine the ⅔ cup of the sugar, cornstarch, flour, and ¼ teaspoon of the salt. Add the milk gradually, stirring constantly with a wire whisk to remove any lumps. Cook over medium heat, stirring constantly, until the mixture thickens and comes to a boil. Continue stirring and boil for 1 minute. Remove from the heat.

5. Gradually stir a few teaspoons of custard into the beaten egg yolks, mixing constantly until blended. When you have added about ½ cup, pour the yolk mixture back into the custard pan, stirring until combined. Cook, stirring constantly, for 2 minutes, until thick and smooth. Remove the pan from the heat.

6. Add the butter to the custard gradually. Stir in 1½ teaspoons of the vanilla. Mix in the toasted flaked coconut.

7. Brush the baked pie shell with the Apricot Glaze. Pour in the filling.

8. Preheat the oven to 375°F.

9. In the large bowl of an electric mixer, beat the egg whites until foamy. Add the cream of tartar and the remaining pinch of salt and beat until soft peaks form. Gradually sprinkle in the remaining ½ cup of sugar, 1 tablespoon at a time, beating well after each addition. When all the sugar has been incorporated, add the remaining 1 teaspoon of vanilla and beat well for 3 to 4 minutes longer, until the meringue forms stiff, shiny peaks. The egg whites should hold their shape and remain moist.

10. Spoon about half of the meringue around the edge of the warm filling. Use a rubber spatula to carefully seal it to the piecrust. Pile the remaining meringue in the center, then spread with the back of a spoon to make decorative swirls. Sprinkle with the remaining ½ cup of untoasted coconut.

11. Bake for 7 to 8 minutes, until the meringue and coconut are golden brown.

12. Cool on a rack in a draft-free place. Serve at room temperature. This pie tastes best when eaten within 3 hours of cooling. Refrigerate any leftover pie.

NOTE: The egg whites in this recipe are not fully cooked. Please see "Egg Information" on page 198.

6 to 8 servings

Lemon Meringue Pie

Who could fail to sing the praises of a billowy tall lemon meringue pie? The tangy, silken lemon base is the perfect counterpoint to the airy cloud of sweet meringue. This pie was the epitome of the American-style haute cuisine that was practiced in New York and Philadelphia in the mid- to late 1800s. Part of the appeal in those days was its expense — the excessive number of eggs, the refined sugar, fresh imported lemons, and sweet creamery butter. Incidentally, if you ever find an old recipe for vinegar pie, you will be looking at a poor man's lemon meringue. In that recipe, cider vinegar and the zest of half a lemon replace the fresh lemons. But we accept no substitutes here: This old-fashioned pie tastes as delectable as ever.

Pastry for a 9-inch single-crust pie (see page 146)	1½ cups water
4 large eggs, separated	½ cup freshly squeezed lemon juice
1¾ cups sugar	2 tablespoons butter, cut into small pieces
6 tablespoons cornstarch	1 tablespoon plus 2 teaspoons finely grated lemon zest
⅛ teaspoon plus 1 pinch salt	½ teaspoon cream of tartar

1. Prepare the pie shell according to the recipe directions. Fully bake the shell (see page 148) and let it cool on a rack before filling.

2. To prepare the lemon filling, beat the egg yolks lightly in a small bowl. Set aside.

3. In the top part of a double boiler, combine 1¼ cups of the sugar, the cornstarch, and ⅛ teaspoon of the salt. Gradually stir in the water and lemon juice. Place the double boiler over (not in) simmering water. Using a whisk, stir the mixture constantly until the sugar is dissolved and the mixture thickens and just comes to a boil. Remove from the heat.

4. Gradually stir a few teaspoons of the mixture into the beaten egg yolks, mixing constantly until blended. When you have added about ½ cup, pour the yolk mixture back into the pan, stirring constantly until combined.

5. Place the pan over the simmering water again. Whisk in the butter gradually, then 1 tablespoon of the lemon zest. Cook the filling over low heat, stirring constantly, for 10 minutes, or until it is thick and smooth. Remove from the heat.

6. Stir the filling to cool slightly, then pour into the baked pie shell.

7. Preheat the oven to 375°F.

8. In the large bowl of an electric mixer, beat the egg whites until foamy. Add the cream of tartar and pinch of salt and beat until soft peaks form. Gradually sprinkle in the remaining ½ cup of sugar, 1 tablespoon at a time, beating well after each addition. When all the sugar has been incorporated, add the remaining 2 teaspoons of lemon zest and beat well for 3 to 4 minutes, until the meringue forms stiff, shiny peaks. The egg whites should hold their shape and remain moist.

9. Spoon about half of the meringue around the edge of the warm filling. Use a rubber spatula to carefully seal it to the piecrust. Pile the remaining meringue in the center, then spread with the back of a spoon to make decorative swirls.

10. Bake for 7 to 8 minutes, until the meringue is golden brown.

11. Cool on a rack in a draft-free place. Serve at room temperature. This pie tastes best when eaten within 3 hours of cooling. Refrigerate any leftover pie.

NOTE: The egg whites in this recipe are not fully cooked. Please see "Egg Information" on page 198.

6 to 8 servings

Part of the secret of success in life is to eat what you like and let the food fight it out inside.

— Mark Twain

Lemon Angel Pie

In the 1940s, *McCall's* magazine ran a recipe for lemon angel pie as a "recipe of the month." The pie has since shown up in many community cookbooks. The title contains the word *angel* because the only way to describe this is "heavenly."

Meringue Pie Shell

4 large egg whites, at room temperature

1 teaspoon freshly squeezed lemon juice

½ teaspoon cream of tartar

¼ teaspoon salt

1 cup sugar

Lemon Filling

4 large egg yolks, at room temperature

¾ cup sugar

⅓ cup freshly squeezed lemon juice

1 tablespoon finely grated lemon zest

⅛ teaspoon salt

1½ cups heavy whipping cream, whipped

6 thin slices lemon, to garnish

1. Preheat the oven to 225°F. Thoroughly grease and flour a 9-inch pie plate.

2. To make the meringue pie shell, beat the egg whites until foamy. Add the lemon juice, cream of tartar, and salt and beat until soft peaks form. Gradually sprinkle in the sugar, 1 tablespoon at a time, beating well after each addition. Continue beating until the meringue is stiff and glossy. Spoon the meringue into the pie plate, building up the sides above the height of the plate to form a bowl. (But don't make the bowl shape wider than the inside dimensions of the pie plate, or the meringue will stick to the edge of the plate.)

3. Bake for 1½ hours, until the meringue has dried and is light tan in color. Turn off the oven, prop open the oven door with a wooden spoon, and let the pie shell remain in the oven until mostly cool, about 1 hour. The meringue shell should be crisp on the outside and slightly soft in the center. Remove from the oven and finish cooling on a wire rack.

4. While the pie shell cools, prepare the filling. In the top of a double boiler, beat the egg yolks with a wire whisk until thick and lemon colored. Place the double boiler over (not in) simmering water. Gradually whisk in the sugar, lemon juice, lemon zest, and salt. Using a metal spoon, stir constantly, until the mixture coats the back of the spoon and is thickened, 8 to 9 minutes. Immediately remove the pan from the double boiler and cool to room temperature. Place a piece of plastic wrap directly on the filling to avoid having a skin form.

5. To assemble the pie, spread half of the whipped cream in the bottom of the meringue shell. Cover with the cooled lemon filling, then top with the remaining whipped cream.

6. Refrigerate for several hours or overnight.

7. Just before serving, garnish the pie with the lemon slices.

6 to 8 servings

With weights and measures just and true,
Oven of even heat,
Well buttered tins and quiet nerves
Success will be complete.

— Anon. from *Cook Book* by Royal Neighbors of America,
Baker Camp No. 2089, Peoria, Ill. (date unknown)

Key Lime Pie

In 1883, Gail Borden applied for a patent on his process of preserving milk. He boiled off the water in the milk in an airtight vacuum pan, similar to those he had seen Shakers use for condensing sweetened fruit juices. The heat process and the added sugar preserved the milk by inhibiting the activity of bacteria. It took consumers many years to trust Borden's condensed milk, the "milk that would stay sweet." But after the Civil War, it was a godsend to the South, where years of battle and plunder had devastated its agricultural base. In Key West, Florida, sweetened condensed milk was not only a sorely needed food, but it was also the inspiration for the famous Key Lime Pie.

Pastry for a 9-inch single-crust pie (see page 146)

3 large eggs, separated

1 can (14 ounces) sweetened condensed milk

1 tablespoon finely grated lime zest

½ cup lime juice (preferably Key lime juice, fresh or bottled; if Key lime juice isn't available, use lime juice freshly squeezed from regular limes)

¼ teaspoon cream of tartar

⅛ teaspoon salt

¼ cup sugar

1 cup heavy whipping cream, whipped (optional)

1. Prepare the pie shell according to the recipe directions. Fully bake the shell (see page 148) and let it cool on a rack before filling.

2. Preheat the oven to 325°F.

3. In a large mixing bowl, beat the egg yolks with a rotary beater or electric mixer for 3 to 4 minutes, until thick and lemon colored. Gradually add the condensed milk, beating until blended. Add the lime zest and lime juice; continue beating until thick and smooth.

4. In another bowl, beat the egg whites until foamy. Add the cream of tartar and salt and beat until soft peaks form. Add the sugar gradually and beat until stiff but not dry. The egg whites should hold their shape and remain moist. Fold the whites into the lime mixture. Spoon the mixture into the pie shell.

5. Bake for 20 minutes, until the filling is set and just beginning to turn golden.

6. Cool on a rack.

7. Refrigerate the pie for 3 to 4 hours, until firm.

8. Just before serving, pipe whipped cream on top or serve the whipped cream separately (if using).

6 to 8 servings

zesty

Zest is the colored part of the rind on a citrus fruit. It does not include the white membranes, which are often bitter. Zest contains essential oils that add a great deal of flavor to a dessert. If a recipe calls for both fresh juice and zest, grate the zest first, then juice the fruit. To finely grate zest, use a zester or the fine-holed side of a box grater. Or strip the zest from the fruit with a zester or swivel-bladed peeler and finely mince.

Coconut Custard Pie

As anyone who has eaten this pie in a diner can attest, it is prone to a soggy crust. Eat this within a few hours of baking, and no one will have any complaints.

Pastry for a 9-inch single-crust pie (see page 146)

1 cup lightly packed, sweetened flaked coconut

4 large eggs

⅔ cup sugar

1½ teaspoons pure vanilla extract

¼ teaspoon salt

⅛ teaspoon grated nutmeg

2½ cups hot (not boiling) milk or half-and-half

1 tablespoon Apricot Glaze (see next page) or 1 tablespoon apple jelly, melted

Freshly grated nutmeg, to garnish

1. Prepare the pie shell according to the recipe directions. Partially bake the shell (see page 148) and let it cool on a rack before filling.

2. Preheat the oven to 300°F with a rack in the lower third of the oven.

3. Spread the coconut on a baking sheet and toast in the oven for 5 to 10 minutes, stirring frequently, until golden brown. Watch carefully to see that the coconut doesn't burn. Remove from the pan and set aside. Increase the oven temperature to 425°F.

4. In a medium-sized bowl, beat the eggs slightly with a whisk. Stir in the sugar, vanilla, salt, and nutmeg. Add the hot milk gradually, stirring constantly. Set aside.

5. Brush the pie shell with the Apricot Glaze, then sprinkle the coconut over the glaze. Place the unfilled pie shell on a shelf in the lower third of the oven. Carefully pour or ladle the custard filling into the shell.

6. Bake for 15 minutes. Reduce the oven temperature to 350°F and bake for 20 minutes longer, or until a knife inserted 1 inch from the outer edge comes out clean. The center may look a little bit soft but will firm up later. Remove from the oven and sprinkle the top with nutmeg.

7. Cool on a wire rack. Serve warm or at room temperature. Refrigerate any leftover pie.

6 to 8 servings

Apricot Glaze

This glaze can be used to seal the bottom crust on fruit pies, top a cake, or glaze fruit on a tart. If you like, serve a dollop of the glaze on top of baked custard.

1 cup apricot preserves
2 tablespoons brandy

1. Combine the preserves and brandy in a small saucepan. Stir over low heat until the jam has melted.
2. Strain and cool. Store extra in the refrigerator for up to 1 month.

1 cup

piecrusts on the run

Piecrusts and pastry dough can be tricky, and preparing them may take more time than a hectic schedule allows. Fortunately, some excellent convenience products are available; an example is ready-to-bake piecrusts in the dairy case.

Frozen piecrusts aren't as high quality as fresh-made ones, and they are prone to breaking while still frozen. Refrigerated pie pastry provides a way around this problem. It is packaged as folded disks of rolled-out pie dough. You simply fit the dough into your pan, crimp the edges, and fill. No one will bother to ask whether you made the crust because it will look and taste homemade – buttery, flaky, and tender.

Basic Piecrust

This recipe makes enough dough for one double-crust pie or two single-crust pie shells. If you need just one pie shell, you can halve the recipe or make two pie shells and freeze the second one.

2½ cups unbleached all-purpose flour

½ teaspoon salt

½ cup (1 stick) butter, cut into small pieces

6 tablespoons vegetable shortening (refrigerate the shortening if you are using a food processor)

6 tablespoons ice water, or more if needed

1. **IF MIXING BY HAND,** combine the flour and salt in a large mixing bowl. With a pastry blender or two knives, cut in the butter. Then add the shortening and combine until the particles are the size of small peas. While stirring lightly and quickly with a fork, sprinkle with the water, 1 tablespoon at a time, just until all the flour is moistened. If the dough doesn't hold together when squeezed, sprinkle with additional water until it holds together and does not crumble. If the dough is sticky, sprinkle with a little more flour. Using the heel of your hand, press portions of the dough flat against your work surface. This will help distribute the fat and make the dough easier to roll out.

   IF MIXING IN A FOOD PROCESSOR, combine the flour and salt in a food processor fitted with a metal blade. Add the butter and shortening and process with on-and-off pulses until the mixture has the consistency of coarse meal. Add 1 tablespoon of ice water through the feed tube, then pulse for 3 seconds. Repeat this start-and-stop procedure with additional tablespoons of water. Process this mixture until it just begins to stick together, but do not allow it to form a ball. Turn out the dough onto a sheet of plastic wrap and pull up on the corners to form a ball.

2. Reshape the dough and flatten it into two disks (if you are making a double-crust pie, make one disk slightly larger than the other) and dust with flour. Wrap separately in plastic wrap. Refrigerate for at least 30 minutes, or up to 4 days.

3. If the dough has been refrigerated for several hours, remove it and leave at room temperature for 15 minutes so it will be easier to handle.

4. On a lightly floured work surface, roll out the dough into a circle, rolling from the center to the edges in even, light strokes. (For a double-crust pie shell, roll out the larger disk first.) Work quickly to handle the dough as little as possible. Roll the dough to a thickness of a little less than ⅛ inch and to a diameter 2 inches larger than the inverted pie plate. Fold the circle in half, lift up, and lay the fold across the center of the pie plate. Unfold and ease the dough loosely into place without stretching it.

5. **FOR A SINGLE-CRUST PIE,** trim the overhanging edge ½ inch larger than the outside rim of the plate. Fold it under, even with the rim of the pie plate, and crimp or flute the edge. Refrigerate the pie shell for 15 minutes, then fill and bake as directed in a recipe or bake unfilled. (See instructions for fully- and partially baked pie shells on next page.)

   FOR A DOUBLE-CRUST PIE, trim the overhanging edge even with the rim of the pie plate. Fill the pie shell with the desired filling. To make the top crust, roll out the remaining dough into a circle about 1 inch larger than the pie plate. Moisten the edge of the bottom crust with water. Fold the dough circle in half, lift off the board, place it across the center of the filled pie, and unfold. Trim the edge ½ inch larger than the pie plate. Tuck the overhang under the edge of the bottom crust. Crimp the edges with a fork or make a fluted pattern with your fingers. Make several decorative slits in the top crust to allow steam to escape. Refrigerate the pie for 15 minutes. Bake as directed in the recipe used.

VARIATION

Sweet Pastry Crust: Add 2 tablespoons of sugar to the flour and salt mixture. For a variation in flavor, use half orange juice and half water for the liquid.

1 double crust for an 8- or 9-inch pie or two 9-inch single crusts

Fully Baked Pie Shell

1. Preheat the oven to 425°F with a rack in the lower third of the oven. Remove the unbaked pie shell (see Basic Pie Crust, pages 146–147) from the refrigerator and prick the bottom and sides of the dough with a fork at ½-inch intervals. Fit a large circle of foil into the bottom and up the sides of the pie dough. Fill it with dried beans or baker's pellets to provide weight and prevent the crust from buckling.

2. Bake in the lower third of the oven for 10 minutes, then remove the foil and beans. Prick the bottom of the crust with a fork again to keep it from puffing up. Return the pie shell to the oven for 10 to 12 minutes, or until it is golden. Cool on a rack before filling.

Partially Baked Pie Shell

1. Preheat the oven to 425°F with a rack in the lower third of the oven. Remove the unbaked pie shell (see Basic Piecrust, pages 146–147) from the refrigerator, but do not prick the crust. Line the pastry with a circle of foil and weight with dried beans or baker's pellets to prevent buckling.

2. Bake in the lower third of the oven for 10 minutes, or until the pastry is set. Remove the foil and beans and bake for 3 to 4 minutes longer, or until the pie shell just begins to set. Cool on a rack before filling.

pie plates

For the best results, select pie plates made of non-shiny darkened metal, anodized aluminum, or heat-proof glass. These pans absorb heat well and help to produce evenly browned piecrusts.

Cream Cheese Pastry

Here's a rich pastry that makes a wonderful single-crust pie shell. Double the recipe if you want a double-crust pie.

1 cup unbleached all-purpose flour

⅛ teaspoon salt

1 package (3 ounces) cream cheese

½ cup (1 stick) butter, cut into small pieces

1. Combine the flour and salt by hand or in a food processor fitted with a steel blade. Add the cream cheese and butter and process, or use a pastry blender to cut in the cream cheese and butter, until the mixture has the consistency of coarse meal.

2. Turn out the dough onto a floured board and knead lightly, just until the dough holds together. Shape the dough into a ball, then flatten into a disk. Dust with flour. Wrap in plastic and refrigerate while you prepare the filling.

3. If the dough has been refrigerated for several hours, remove it from the refrigerator and leave at room temperature for 15 minutes so it will be easier to handle.

4. On a lightly floured work surface, roll out the dough into a circle, rolling from center to edge in even, light strokes. Work quickly to handle the dough as little as possible. Roll the dough to a thickness of a little less than ⅛ inch and to a diameter 2 inches larger than the inverted pie plate. Fold the circle in half, lift off the board, and lay the fold across the center of the pie plate or tart pan. Unfold and ease the dough loosely into place without stretching it.

5. Trim the overhanging edge ½ inch larger than the outside rim of the plate. Fold it under, even with the rim of the pie plate, and crimp or flute the edge. Refrigerate the pie shell for 15 minutes.

6. Fill and bake as directed in a recipe or bake unfilled.

7. Follow instructions on page 148 for a fully- or partially baked pie shell.

1 single-crust pie shell

Graham Cracker Crust

To save time, some people don't bother to bake crumb crusts. But we find that baking results in a pie that is less soggy, cuts better, and has a nice toasty flavor.

1½ cups finely ground graham cracker crumbs

3 tablespoons sugar

6 tablespoons (¾ stick) butter, melted

¼ teaspoon ground cinnamon

1. Preheat the oven to 350°F. Lightly grease an 8- or 9-inch pie plate or springform pan.
2. Combine the graham cracker crumbs, sugar, butter, and cinnamon. Press firmly onto the bottom and up the sides of the pan.
3. Bake for 8 minutes, then set aside on a rack to cool before filling.

NOTE: It takes about 10½ sheets of graham crackers (each sheet has four individual crackers) to make 1½ cups of crumbs. Graham cracker crumbs are easily made in a food processor.

8- or 9-inch pie shell

Chocolate Crumb Crust

1¾ cups finely ground chocolate wafer crumbs (about 35 wafers)

5 tablespoons (about ⅔ stick) butter, melted

1. Preheat the oven to 350°F. Lightly grease an 8- or 9-inch pie plate or springform pan.
2. Combine the crumbs and melted butter. Press firmly onto the bottom and up the sides of the pan.
3. Bake for 8 minutes, then set aside on a rack to cool before filling.

9- or 10-inch pie shell

4 · Fruit Desserts

Ambrosia

For a very attractive presentation, serve this ambrosia in a glass dish to display the colorful layers of fruit.

4 large navel or seedless oranges

½ cup freshly squeezed orange juice or pineapple juice (see Note below)

Confectioners' sugar

2 cups diced fresh or canned pineapple

1 tablespoon chopped fresh mint (optional)

¾ cup lightly packed, sweetened flaked coconut

2 tablespoons orange liqueur (Grand Marnier) or brandy (optional)

1. With a vegetable peeler, remove the zest of one of the oranges. Cut it into very fine julienne. Slice off the white membrane of that orange. Peel the remaining three oranges, removing all the white membrane. Over a bowl to catch the juice, section the oranges or cut them into ½-inch wedges, placing them in a separate dish. Mix ¼ cup of the juice, the julienned orange zest, and a little confectioners' sugar to sweeten the fruit, if needed.

2. In another bowl, combine the pineapple with the mint (if using), and the remaining ¼ cup of juice. Sweeten to taste with confectioners' sugar.

3. Set aside 2 tablespoons of the coconut. In a serving bowl, alternate layers of oranges and pineapple, sprinkling each layer with coconut. Drizzle in the orange liqueur (if using) and the juice in which the fruits have macerated. Refrigerate for several hours.

4. Sprinkle with the reserved coconut and serve.

NOTE: If you are using canned pineapple packed in pineapple juice, you can use that juice instead of the orange juice. This recipe has tremendous flexibility and need not be followed to the letter.

VARIATIONS

Substitute mandarin oranges for the navel oranges. You can also add sliced bananas, but they should be mixed in just before serving because they brown easily.

4 to 6 servings

food of the gods

Many of our fruit desserts originated in colonial America. These cobblers and crisps were most often made from apples and berries, which were homegrown or gathered in the wild. Not so with ambrosia, a dessert that originated in the South in the nineteenth century, when coconut and oranges could be purchased at stores. The recipe made its first appearance in print in an 1879 cookbook of recipes from Virginia, where it was a simple combination of oranges, sugar, and coconut. More elaborate versions soon evolved, permitting the addition of pineapple and bananas and sometimes even sour cream, marshmallows, and dates. Today, it is acceptable to include any fruit you choose; just be sure to top the dessert with coconut if you want to call it ambrosia.

Apple Crisp

Apple crisp, apple crunch, apple delight — there were, and are, many names for (and variations of) this dessert with an apple pie filling and a crunchy topping, and many variations. This sort of dessert was widespread in early American kitchens because it was perfect to make with the less-than-perfect apples that were dug up from bins in the root cellar. After all the wormholes and bruises were cut away, baked apples were out of the question, but apple crisp, crunch, delight was just the thing.

Filling

- 3 pounds tart apples, peeled, cored, and sliced (about 7 cups)
- ¼ cup granulated sugar
- 1 tablespoon finely grated lemon zest
- 1 tablespoon freshly squeezed lemon juice
- 1 teaspoon ground cinnamon
- ½ teaspoon freshly grated nutmeg

Topping

- ½ cup firmly packed dark brown sugar
- ½ cup ground cookie or graham cracker crumbs (see Note)
- ½ cup unbleached all-purpose flour
- ½ cup (1 stick) butter, at room temperature
- ⅓ cup chopped almonds
- Cream, whipped cream, or ice cream, to serve (optional)

1. Preheat the oven to 350°F. Lightly grease a 9-inch square baking dish or a deep 9-inch pie plate.

2. Combine the apples in a large bowl with the granulated sugar, lemon zest, lemon juice, cinnamon, and nutmeg. Toss to mix. Transfer the apples to the baking dish, pressing down on them so that they're level with the top of the dish.

3. To make the topping, in the same bowl that held the apples, combine the brown sugar, cookie crumbs, and flour. With your fingers, rub the butter into the crumb mixture until it resembles coarse meal. Mix in the almonds. Sprinkle the topping over the apples, pressing it down and making sure the edges of the apples are covered.

4. Bake for 45 minutes, or until the top is browned and the apples are tender when tested with a fork.

5. Serve warm or chilled with cream (if using).

NOTE: For ½ cup ground cookie crumbs, you will need approximately eight gingersnaps or 11 vanilla wafers. For ½ cup graham cracker crumbs, use about 3½ sheets, or 14 individual crackers.

6 servings

In short, if you wish to avail yourself of the blessings of a bountiful Providence, which are within your reach, you must plant an orchard. And when you do it, see that you plant good fruit. The best are cheapest.

— McCall's Home Cook Book and General Guide,
compiled by Mrs. Jennie Harlan
(New York: The McCall Company, 1890)

Apple Brown Betty

This is one of the simplest of the fruit desserts, and we have no idea how the name originated. The walnuts add extra flavor and texture.

1 cup dry unseasoned bread crumbs

¼ cup granulated sugar

⅓ cup (about ⅔ stick) butter, melted

5 cups peeled and sliced apples (5 to 6 medium-sized apples)

½ cup firmly packed light or dark brown sugar

½ cup chopped walnuts

1 teaspoon ground cinnamon

½ teaspoon freshly grated nutmeg

Zest and juice of 1 lemon

Cream, whipped cream, or ice cream, to serve (optional)

1. Preheat the oven to 350°F. Lightly butter a 1½-quart baking dish.

2. In a medium-sized bowl, combine the bread crumbs with the granulated sugar and butter. Pat half of the mixture into the bottom of the baking dish.

3. In another bowl, combine the apples, brown sugar, walnuts, cinnamon, nutmeg, and lemon zest and juice. Spread over the crumb mixture. Top with the remaining crumb mixture.

4. Cover and bake for 40 minutes. Remove the cover, increase the heat to 400°F, and bake for 10 minutes longer.

5. Serve warm with cream (if using).

6 servings

a is for apple

From a cook's point of view, it would be nice if the best eating apples were also the best cooking apples. Then you could conduct your own taste test, stock up on your favorite eating apple, and know that whenever the mood strikes for apple pie or crisp, you've got the right ingredients.

When new apple varieties are developed, they are rigorously tested for cooking characteristics because there are no hard-and-fast rules for which varieties cook best. Juicy apples don't necessary become watery when cooked, though some, like McIntosh, do. Sweet apples don't necessarily stay sweet when cooked, though some, like Newton Pippins, do. Some, like Red Delicious, become bland and flat-tasting. Apples that make a great sauce, like Braeburns, may be poor choices for making pie.

For making pies and crisps, nothing beats a Northern Spy, which is one of those formerly popular, now disappearing varieties. Jonagolds, Jonathans, and Rhode Island Greenings make great pies. Golden Delicious, paired with a tart variety, such as Granny Smith or McIntosh, is terrific in pies and crisps. For sauce, most people use a mix of what hasn't been used in baking or eating fresh and will make up with sugar and cinnamon whatever the apple doesn't provide. Sauce makers, as a rule, recommend Braeburn, Gala, Golden Delicious, Granny Smith, Jonagold, Jonathan, Newtown Pippin, and Winesap. Cortlands are an excellent choice for salads because of their remarkably white flesh. Golden Delicious holds its color well, too. Cortlands dry well, as do Galas and Winesaps. When in doubt, choose Golden Delicious or Jonagold. Both are excellent, all-purpose apples.

Apple Charlotte

This dessert, something of a fancy variation on Apple Brown Betty, has French origins. It was supposedly named after one Charlotte Buff, on whom Johann Wolfgang von Goethe based the heroine of *Die Leiden des Jungens Werthers,* a very popular novel in its day (1774). The first published recipe for apple charlotte might be the one that appeared in *American Domestic Cookery,* by Maria Eliza Rundell, in 1823.

Charlotte

¾ cup (1½ sticks) butter

3½ to 4 pounds tart apples, peeled, cored, and sliced ¼ inch thick (about 8 cups sliced)

2 tablespoons water

¾ to 1 cup firmly packed light brown sugar

1 tablespoon finely grated lemon zest

2 tablespoons freshly squeezed lemon juice

2 teaspoons ground cinnamon

¼ teaspoon freshly grated nutmeg

12 to 14 slices firm white bread, crusts removed, thinly sliced

Whipped cream, to serve

Rum Apricot Sauce

1 cup apricot jam

1 tablespoon water

3 tablespoons dark rum

1. Lightly grease a 2-quart charlotte mold, soufflé dish, or straight-sided glass baking dish.

2. In a large skillet, melt ¼ cup of the butter over medium heat. Add the apples and water and cook, covered, stirring occasionally, until the liquid just begins to boil, 5 to 8 minutes. Stir in ¾ cup of the brown sugar, the lemon zest, and the lemon juice. Cook, uncovered, until the apples are softened and glazed, 5 to 10 minutes. All the liquid should be absorbed. Mix in the cinnamon and nutmeg. Taste and add more brown sugar if needed. Set aside.

3. Preheat the oven to 375°F.

4. Melt the remaining ½ cup of butter. Cut three or more slices of bread into narrow triangles (like slices of pie) to fit the bottom of the mold. The points should meet in the center and fan out like the spokes of a wheel. Brush both sides of the bread with the melted butter and arrange in the bottom of the mold. Cut six or more slices of the remaining bread in half lengthwise. Brush both sides of each rectangle with butter; line the sides of the mold with bread, standing the slices upright and overlapping them slightly. With a slotted spoon, transfer the apple mixture to the prepared baking dish. Brush the remaining bread with butter and trim to fit over the apples. Tap the mold on the work surface and gently press down the bread. Trim excess bread from around the edge until it is flush with the top of the apple charlotte.

5. Bake for 30 minutes, press down the apples, and bake for 15 minutes longer, or until the top is golden brown. Trim the bread again from around the top edge, if necessary.

6. Let cool on a rack for 15 minutes while you prepare the sauce.

7. In a small saucepan, combine the apricot jam and water. Stir over low heat until the jam is melted. Simmer, stirring occasionally, for 3 minutes. Remove from the heat and strain. Blend in the rum. Let cool slightly.

8. To serve, carefully loosen the charlotte by running a knife around the inside of the mold. Invert it onto a serving dish and brush with warm apricot sauce. Pour some of the sauce around the base of the charlotte. Serve warm with the whipped cream.

8 to 10 servings

Apple Pandowdy

A pandowdy is a cross between a pie and a pudding. It starts with a crust that is chopped up until it disappears into the fruit — a step that is called "dowdying." With a filling that includes butter and a little cream, a pandowdy is richer than your average pie. This old-fashioned dessert is obviously for those of us with old-fashioned work habits. Serve after a hard day of gardening, chopping wood, or running a marathon.

Pastry

1¼ cups unbleached all-purpose flour

⅓ cup cornmeal, preferably stone-ground

2 tablespoons sugar

¼ teaspoon salt

6 tablespoons butter, chilled

¼ cup vegetable shortening

Approximately ¼ cup ice water

Apple Filling

6 cups peeled and sliced apples (6 to 8 apples)

1½ teaspoons ground cinnamon

½ teaspoon ground mace

⅓ cup plus 2 tablespoons pure maple syrup

6 tablespoons butter, melted

¼ cup apple cider or juice

¼ cup light cream

1. To make the pastry, combine the flour, cornmeal, sugar, and salt in a medium-sized bowl or in a food processor. Cut in the butter and shortening until the mixture resembles coarse crumbs. Add just enough ice water to allow the mixture to hold together. Divide into two balls and flatten into disks. Refrigerate while you prepare the filling.

2. Preheat the oven to 400°F. Lightly butter a 1½-quart baking dish.

3. To prepare the filling, in a large bowl combine the apples, cinnamon, mace, ⅓ cup of the maple syrup, and 4 tablespoons of the butter.

4. On a lightly floured work surface, roll out one piece of dough about ⅛ inch thick to fit into the baking dish. Transfer the dough to the dish and trim the uneven edges. The dough should fit up the sides of the baking dish, but don't worry if it doesn't. Spoon the apples into the baking dish, scraping out the syrup and butter from the bottom of the bowl. Roll out the second piece of dough and fit it over the apples. Seal against the sides of the dish.

5. Bake for about 10 minutes. Remove the pandowdy from the oven and reduce the heat to 325°F. Using a sharp knife or a chopper, cut the crust into the fruit, until the crust has almost disappeared into the fruit. Combine the apple cider, cream, the remaining 2 tablespoons of maple syrup, and the remaining 2 tablespoons of melted butter. Pour over the top. Return the pandowdy to the oven and continue to bake for 45 to 50 minutes, until the fruit is tender.

6. Serve warm.

6 servings

Apple Dumplings

Apple dumplings take a little more time than some of the other desserts in this chapter, but they can be assembled hours ahead and kept in the refrigerator until baking time. The baked dumplings don't keep well, so make only as many as you plan to serve and bake just before serving.

Pastry

- 2 cups unbleached all-purpose flour
- 2 tablespoons sugar
- ½ teaspoon salt
- ½ cup (1 stick) butter, chilled, cut into small pieces
- ¼ cup vegetable shortening
- 4 to 6 tablespoons ice water
- 1 egg white, slightly beaten with 1 teaspoon water

Filling

- 6 large baking apples
- ¼ cup (½ stick) butter, at room temperature
- ¼ cup raspberry or blackberry preserves
- ¼ cup chopped almonds
- 2 teaspoons finely grated orange zest
- Whipped cream or ice cream, to serve (optional)

1. Preheat the oven to 400°F. Lightly butter a large shallow baking dish.

2. To make the pastry, combine the flour, sugar, and salt in a medium-sized bowl or in a food processor. Cut in the butter and shortening until the mixture resembles coarse crumbs. Add just enough of the ice water, 1 tablespoon at a time, until the mixture holds together. Divide the pastry dough into six cubes and flatten into square disks. Refrigerate them while you prepare the filling.

3. To prepare the filling, peel the apples and core about three quarters of the way down. Trim the bottoms, if necessary, to enable the apples to stand.

4. Beat together the butter and preserves. Mix in the almonds and orange zest. Stuff into the apple centers.

5. On a lightly floured work surface, roll out each pastry disk to a square of approximately 6 inches. Brush with the egg white and center an apple on each square. Bring up the dough over the apple and press the edges together, using the egg white mixture if needed to make them stick. If you want to get fancy, use scraps of dough to make apple leaves, and affix them on top of the dumplings with the egg white mixture. Place in the prepared baking dish.

6. Chill for 3 to 5 minutes in the freezer (or for several hours in the refrigerator).

7. Bake for 45 minutes, until the pastry tops are golden brown.

8. Serve warm with the whipped cream or ice cream (if using).

6 servings

In one word, Queequeg, said I, rather digressively; hell is an idea first born on an undigested apple dumpling; and since then perpetrated through the hereditary dyspepsias nurtured by Ramadans.

— Herman Melville, *Moby-Dick* (1851)

Baked Apples

Consider this a crustless apple pie — very easy to make.

6 large Rome Beauty or other baking apples

¼ cup firmly packed light brown sugar

2 tablespoons toasted slivered almonds (optional)

2 tablespoons dried currants

2 tablespoons golden raisins

1 tablespoon finely grated lemon zest

1 teaspoon ground cinnamon

½ teaspoon freshly grated nutmeg

2 tablespoons butter, cut into pieces

1½ cups apple juice or cider, heated

2 teaspoons granulated sugar

Light or heavy whipping cream, to serve (optional)

1. Preheat the oven to 375°F.

2. Core the apples to ½ inch from the bottom. Remove a 1-inch strip of skin around the top of each apple. Stand the apples upright in a shallow baking dish that will hold them compactly.

3. Mix the brown sugar, almonds (if using), currants, raisins, and lemon zest. Fill the apple centers evenly with the mixture. Sprinkle with cinnamon and nutmeg. Dot with the butter. Pour the hot apple juice around the apples to a depth of ½ inch.

4. Bake for 45 to 60 minutes, basting frequently, until the apples are tender when pierced with a fork. Sprinkle the granulated sugar over the apples during the last 5 minutes of baking. (The baking time will depend upon the variety and size of the apples.)

5. Serve warm or at room temperature in dessert dishes; spoon the juices remaining in the baking dish over the apples. Top with the cream (if using).

VARIATION

The currants and raisins can be plumped in apple brandy or sherry for several hours before you fill the apples.

6 servings

Bananas Foster

Bananas Foster was created for a Richard Foster, owner of the Foster Awning Company, at Brennan's Restaurant in New Orleans sometime in the 1950s as part of a "Breakfast at Brennan's" advertising campaign. The dish became so popular that it has been claimed by the city of New Orleans as a traditional dessert.

1 pint vanilla ice cream	½ cup firmly packed brown sugar
4 firm ripe bananas	2 tablespoons freshly squeezed orange juice
4 tablespoons butter	¾ cup dark or light rum (dark has more flavor)

1. Place a scoop of ice cream onto each of four dessert plates. (If you prefer, scoop the ice cream ahead and place the plates in the freezer. Keep frozen until 5 to 10 minutes before serving.)

2. Peel the bananas. Cut them into halves lengthwise, then into halves again cutting crosswise.

3. To make the sauce, melt the butter over medium heat in a large skillet. Add the sugar and orange juice and cook, stirring, until the sauce is bubbly and smooth. Add the bananas and sauté for 3 to 5 minutes, basting the bananas with the sauce until the bananas are nicely coated. Remove from the heat and keep warm.

4. Heat the rum in a small saucepan just until warm. Ignite with a match and pour the flaming liquor over the bananas. Rotate the pan back and forth until the flames subside. (If you have a fan over the stove, make sure it is off before you attempt to do this.)

5. Spoon the bananas and sauce over the ice cream and serve at once.

4 servings

Berry Cobbler

The term *cobbler* is probably derived from an old Middle English word that means "to lump together." It also means, according to Webster, "to make or do clumsily or unhandily." Well, this lumped-together dish of biscuit and fruit tastes lovely, no matter what its name and despite its homely appearance. The rough, uneven surface of the biscuit topping has always reminded us of cobblestones.

Berry Filling

- 6 cups fresh blackberries, boysenberries, raspberries, blueberries, or a combination of berries
- 3 tablespoons unbleached all-purpose flour
- ½ cup sugar, or to taste
- 2 teaspoons finely grated orange zest
- 1 tablespoon freshly squeezed orange juice
- 2 tablespoons butter, cut into small pieces

Biscuit Dough Topping

- 1 cup unbleached all-purpose flour
- 3 tablespoons sugar
- 1½ teaspoons baking powder
- ¼ teaspoon salt
- 4 tablespoons butter, chilled
- 1 tablespoon vegetable shortening
- ¼ to ⅓ cup milk or half-and-half
- Cream, to serve

1. To make the berry filling, stem and gently rinse the berries. Drain on paper towels. Transfer to an 8-inch square baking dish or 1½-quart casserole.

2. In a small bowl, combine the flour, sugar, orange zest, and orange juice. Toss with the berries, mixing gently until they are thoroughly coated. If the berries are particularly tart, add more sugar to taste. Dot with the butter.

3. Set aside the filling for 30 minutes or refrigerate for several hours. Bring to room temperature before baking.

4. Preheat the oven to 400°F.

5. To make the biscuit dough, sift the flour, 2 tablespoons of the sugar, the baking powder, and salt into a bowl or food processor. Cut 3 tablespoons of the butter and the shortening into the flour mixture until it has the consistency of coarse crumbs. Add ¼ cup of the milk all at once and stir with a fork or pulse the machine briefly just until the dough comes together, adding more milk if necessary.

6. Turn out the dough onto a lightly floured work surface. Knead lightly 12 to 15 times, sprinkling with a little flour if the dough is sticky. (Biscuit dough can be refrigerated for up to 2 hours before baking.)

7. Press out the dough gently into a shape that will be large enough to cover the berries. Transfer the dough carefully to the baking dish, crimping the edges around the dish.

8. Melt the remaining 1 tablespoon of butter. Brush the top of the dough with the melted butter. Sprinkle with the remaining 1 tablespoon of sugar. With the tip of a sharp knife, cut three or four vents in the top of the dough to allow steam to escape.

9. Bake for 35 to 40 minutes, until the biscuit topping is golden.

10. Serve warm with a spoonful of cream topping each serving.

6 servings

You may make houses enchantingly beautiful, hang them with pictures, have them clean and airy and convenient; but if the stomach is fed with sour bread and burnt meats, it will raise such rebellions that the eyes will see no beauty anywhere.

— *The House-keepers Manual* by Catherine E. Beecher and Harriet Beecher Stowe (Cincinnati: J. B. Ford & Co., 1874)

blueberries

The high-bush blueberry is charming. It grows, thorn-free, to convenient picking heights. Its plump, dusky blue berries glisten like jewels in the morning dew. We have picked such berries at pick-your-own farms, stripping a bush with clumsy fingers and filling buckets in minutes. It was easy — too easy, in fact.

No high-bush blueberry can compare to the taste of a wild low-bush blueberry. Picking these tiny berries that grow on ankle-high shrubs is hard labor. Professionals — meaning those seasonal workers who are paid for their efforts with cash, not muffins — use a rake to strip the low-growing shrubs of the berries. But the work is backbreaking and yields are relatively low. Most of the commercial harvest goes into commercial baking, where the small berries are prized for muffins. Still, some of the wild blueberry crops make it to farm stands and fruit markets in New England.

"Wild" is something of a misnomer. The berries are wild only insofar as the fields are not planted by the farmer. But they are managed. After harvest each year, the farmer burns the fields to eliminate weeds. Underground, the blueberry rhizomes remain intact, ready to spread to the newly cleared fields. Birds help the process by dropping seeds on the cleared land. By July, new growth is evident in the fields. By the second year, blueberries blossom and set tiny, sweet, deliciously fragrant fruits. This is the fruit that shouldn't be missed.

Blueberry Grunt

One can easily imagine how this recipe came about. On a hot August day in Maine, a cook, planning to make a blueberry shortcake, decided it was just too hot to fire up the woodstove for the shortcake biscuits. Instead, she put the blueberries in a pot with some sugar and water and steamed the biscuit dough like dumplings, hoping for the best.

You may also hope for the best when you see the gluey-looking biscuits. But this dessert is an absolute favorite. Serve it up in the kitchen in dessert bowls and cover with a slosh of unsweetened cream. The flavor, the contrast of textures — it's divine.

6 cups fresh or unsweetened frozen blueberries

1 cup water

1½ cups sugar

½ teaspoon ground cinnamon

1¾ cups unbleached all-purpose flour

1 tablespoon baking powder

½ teaspoon salt

6 tablespoons butter, chilled

Approximately ¾ cup milk

Cream

1. In a 9- or 10-inch nonreactive skillet, combine the berries, water, sugar, and cinnamon. Bring to a boil, reduce the heat, and simmer for 10 minutes. Remove from the heat while you prepare the biscuit dough.

2. Sift together the flour, baking powder, and salt into a medium-sized mixing bowl or food processor. Cut in the butter until the mixture resembles coarse crumbs. Add the milk and mix just enough to combine. The dough will be lumpy.

3. Drop the dough by the spoonful over the berries.

4. Cover tightly and steam for 15 to 20 minutes, keeping the heat just high enough to allow the berries to bubble.

5. Serve warm in bowls with a little cream poured over each serving.

6 servings

Berry Fool

So easy even a fool can make this? Or a variation on the French word *feuillet,* which means layer? This dessert is an easily prepared blending of fruit and whipped cream. Simple and sublime.

2 cups sliced fresh or frozen strawberries, whole raspberries, or gooseberries

¼ cup sugar

3 tablespoons water

2 teaspoons freshly squeezed lemon juice

1 cup heavy whipping cream

1 tablespoon Kirsch, fraise des bois, or cherry brandy

⅓ cup toasted macaroon crumbs, to garnish

1. In a small saucepan, combine the berries, sugar, and water. Bring to a boil, reduce the heat, and simmer for 4 to 5 minutes, until the juices become syrupy.

2. Pour the berries into a bowl, cover, and refrigerate for 2 hours, or until the berries are very cold.

3. Purée the berries and the lemon juice in a food processor or blender. If you are using raspberries, press the berries through a sieve, collecting as much pulp and juice as possible and discarding the seeds.

4. Whip the cream until soft peaks form, then add the liqueur and beat until stiff. Fold the cream into the berry purée.

5. To serve, spoon the berry mixture into six dessert dishes or a 1-quart serving dish. Sprinkle with the macaroon crumbs. Serve immediately or cover with plastic and refrigerate for several hours.

NOTE: If you are using frozen sweetened fruit, defrost and reserve the juice. Heat the juice to boiling and cook until the syrup is reduced to 3 tablespoons. Use the reduced juice in place of the water and eliminate the sugar.

6 servings

Cherry Crunch

Here the cherries are sandwiched between two coarse-textured, brown sugar pastry layers. In the finished dish, the cherries appear as bumps pressing up on the crust.

2 cups drained and pitted canned cherries (reserve ½ cup cherry juice) or 2 cups defrosted frozen cherries, drained (reserve juice and add enough grape or orange juice to make ½ cup)

1½ tablespoons quick-cooking tapioca

1 cup firmly packed light brown sugar

1 cup unbleached all-purpose flour

¼ teaspoon baking powder

¼ teaspoon baking soda

¼ teaspoon salt

1 cup rolled oats (not instant)

½ cup (1 stick) butter, at room temperature

½ cup chopped walnuts

¼ teaspoon almond extract

Cream, whipped cream, or vanilla ice cream, to serve (optional)

1. In a small bowl, mix the cherry juice with the tapioca, stirring to combine. Set aside for 15 minutes.

2. Preheat the oven to 350°F. Lightly butter a 9-inch square baking dish.

3. In a medium-sized bowl, combine the brown sugar, flour, baking powder, baking soda, and salt. Stir in the oats. With your fingertips, rub the butter into the flour mixture until it resembles coarse meal. Stir in the walnuts.

4. Press half of the crumb mixture into the bottom of the baking dish. Arrange the cherries over it. Add the almond extract to the tapioca mixture and spoon it over the cherries. Cover the fruit with the remaining crumb mixture.

5. Bake for 35 to 40 minutes, until golden brown.

6. Serve warm or chilled with cream (if using).

6 servings

Peach Slump

Many of our heritage fruit dessert recipes are variations on a single theme — fruit and biscuit dough — and this slump is no exception. Here, peaches are baked under a biscuit topping, but then the dessert is inverted onto a serving plate so the fruit can "slump" into the pastry. You can further the slumping process by whacking the fruit with a spoon, as some recipes recommend, but we prefer to skip that step. Serve this as soon as possible after you remove it from the oven. After sitting around for a couple of hours, the biscuit dough becomes pasty. Nectarines or apples can be substituted for the peaches.

8 cups thinly sliced peeled peaches (approximately 8 medium-sized peaches)

2 tablespoons light brown sugar

½ teaspoon ground cinnamon

½ teaspoon almond extract

1½ cups unbleached all-purpose flour

2 teaspoons baking powder

2 tablespoons granulated sugar

6 tablespoons butter, chilled

½ cup milk

¼ cup buttermilk or plain yogurt

1 egg, well beaten

1. Preheat the oven to 400°F. Lightly butter a 1½-quart baking dish.

2. In a medium-sized bowl, toss together the peaches, brown sugar, cinnamon, and almond extract. Spread in the bottom of the baking dish.

3. Sift together the flour, baking powder, and granulated sugar into a medium-sized bowl or food processor. Cut in the butter with two knives or by pulsating the food processor on and off, until the mixture has the consistency of coarse crumbs. Combine the milk, buttermilk, and egg. Add to the flour mixture and mix briefly. Do not knead; the dough will be sticky, stiff, and lumpy.

4. Drop the dough by the spoonful over the peaches. Try to get even coverage, but don't worry about a few bare spots.

We'd love your thoughts . . .

Your reactions, criticisms, things you did or didn't like about this Storey Book. Please use space below (or write a letter if you'd prefer
— even send photos!) telling how you've made use of the information . . . how you've put it to work . . . the more details the better!

Thanks in advance for your help in building our library of good Storey Books.

Book Title: _____

Purchased From: _____

Comments: _____

_____

_____

_____

_____

_____

Pamela B. Art

President, Storey Books

Your Name: _____

Mailing Address: _____
(Please Print)

E-mail Address: _____

☐ You have my permission to quote from my comments and use these quotations in ads, brochures, mail, and other promotions used
to market Storey Books.

To order this book or any Storey title CALL 800-441-5700 or visit our web site at www.storey.com

Signed _____ Date _____

e-mail: feedback@storey.com   website: www.storey.com   PRINTED IN THE UNITED STATES

1/03

From: _____

BUSINESS REPLY MAIL

FIRST-CLASS MAIL   PERMIT NO. 10   N. ADAMS MA

POSTAGE WILL BE PAID BY ADDRESSEE

STOREY BOOKS

PO Box 206

North Adams MA 01247-9919

5. Bake for about 25 minutes, until the top is golden and the juices are bubbling.

6. Cool on a wire rack for about 5 minutes. Then loosen the biscuit from the sides of the pan and invert onto a serving platter. Serve warm.

4 to 6 servings

peach history

The peach has made a very successful journey from China to the New World. Actually, it went from China to Persia to Rome and then spread throughout Europe. The fruit bore the name *Persian apple,* which in Middle English became *peche.* The Spanish brought the peach to the New World in the seventeenth century.

Raspberry Buckle

In buckles, the fruit is covered by a cake layer, which has a tendency to buckle and crack as it bakes. No problem: The crumb topping hides all while the cake layer becomes permeated with the flavor of raspberries. This is a casual sort of dessert, good to serve at brunch or whenever you might serve a coffee cake.

Berries

6 cups fresh or frozen unsweetened raspberries

½ cup sugar

1 tablespoon freshly squeezed lemon juice

Cake

2½ cups sifted unbleached all-purpose flour

1½ teaspoons baking powder

½ teaspoon baking soda

¼ teaspoon salt

⅛ teaspoon freshly grated nutmeg

10 tablespoons (1¼ sticks) butter, at room temperature

1⅓ cups granulated sugar

3 large eggs

1 cup buttermilk or ½ cup plain yogurt and ½ cup milk, at room temperature

1 teaspoon almond extract

Topping

½ cup unbleached all-purpose flour

½ cup firmly packed brown sugar

½ teaspoon ground cinnamon

4 tablespoons butter, at room temperature

¾ cup sliced almonds

1. Preheat the oven to 350°F. Grease a 9-inch by 13-inch baking dish.

2. To prepare the berries, combine them with the sugar and lemon juice in a saucepan. Heat over low heat until the sugar dissolves. Spoon into the prepared baking dish.

3. To make the cake, sift together the flour, baking powder, baking soda, salt, and nutmeg. Sift two more times. Set aside.

4. In the large bowl of an electric mixer, cream the butter and sugar until light and fluffy. Add the eggs, one at a time, beating well after each addition. Add one third of the buttermilk alternately with one third of the flour mixture, beating well after each addition. Continue adding the buttermilk and flour in thirds until the batter is smooth. Stir in the almond extract. Pour the batter over the raspberries.

5. Bake for 25 to 30 minutes, or until the center of the cake is set but still soft.

6. To make the topping, while the cake bakes, combine the flour, brown sugar, and cinnamon. With your fingers, rub the butter into the crumb mixture until it resembles coarse meal. Toss in the almonds. Sprinkle the mixture on top of the partially baked cake.

7. Continue baking for 15 to 20 minutes, until a tester inserted into the cake layer comes out clean.

8. Serve warm or cool, directly out of the pan.

10 to 12 servings

Raspberry Trifle

Did this taste any better when it was known as Tipsy Parson? This English dessert is a favorite no matter where it is served, no matter what it is called.

Custard

4 large egg yolks

¼ cup sugar

2 tablespoons cornstarch

Pinch of salt

2½ cups hot (not boiling) milk

2 tablespoons brandy

1 cup heavy whipping cream

Cake and Fruit

1 pound cake (12 ounces) or sponge cake

½ cup raspberry jam

½ to ⅔ cup cream sherry

2 packages (10 ounces each) frozen raspberries, thawed and drained, or 2 cups fresh raspberries, sweetened with sugar to taste, and drained

Garnish

1 cup heavy whipping cream

2 tablespoons sifted confectioners' sugar

¼ teaspoon almond extract

½ cup toasted slivered almonds

¼ cup fresh raspberries

1. To make the custard, in the top part of a double boiler, beat the egg yolks with a wire whisk until thick and lemon colored. Mix in the sugar, cornstarch, and salt. Place over simmering water. Gradually add the milk and cook, stirring constantly, until the mixture thickens and coats a metal spoon.

2. Remove the custard from the heat. Stir in 1 tablespoon of the brandy. Cover the surface of the custard with plastic wrap and place the bowl in a pan of ice water until chilled, stirring occasionally.

3. Whip the cream until stiff. Stir in the remaining 1 tablespoon of brandy, then fold into the cold custard.

4. To assemble the trifle, cut the cake into ¼-inch slices (18 to 20 slices). Spread a layer of jam on half the cake slices, then sandwich the slices together. Using a pastry brush, soak both sides of the cake sandwiches with the sherry, then cut them into four equal pieces. Arrange half of the cake sandwiches over the bottom and partway up the sides of the bowl. Spoon on half of the berries. Spread half of the custard over the berries. Repeat the layers with the remaining cake pieces, berries, and custard.

5. Cover the trifle with plastic wrap and refrigerate for several hours, or for up to 2 days.

6. Before serving, whip the cream for the garnish until soft peaks form. Add the confectioners' sugar and almond extract and beat until stiff. Pipe the whipped cream on top of the trifle. Sprinkle the toasted almonds over the top and garnish with the fresh raspberries. Serve in dessert dishes.

16 servings

Rhubarb Rolypoly

Here is an old-fashioned dessert that wraps rhubarb in a tender biscuit dough and bakes it in a sweet, spicy syrup. This is at its best served warm with a dollop of cream. It makes a fine dish for brunch or dessert. Thinly sliced apples are often used instead of rhubarb.

Syrup

1½ cups sugar

1½ cups water

1½ teaspoons ground cinnamon

⅛ grated teaspoon nutmeg

Filling

2 pounds fresh rhubarb or 6 cups defrosted frozen unsweetened rhubarb

1 tablespoon sugar

1 teaspoon finely grated orange zest

Biscuit Dough

2 cups unbleached all-purpose flour

¼ cup sugar

2 teaspoons baking powder

2 teaspoons finely grated orange zest

½ teaspoon salt

6 tablespoons butter, chilled, cut into small pieces

1 large egg

Milk

1 tablespoon butter, melted

1. Preheat the oven to 400°F. Butter a 9- by 13-inch baking dish.

2. To make the syrup, in a medium-sized saucepan combine the sugar with the water, cinnamon, and nutmeg. Bring to a boil. Reduce the heat and simmer for 5 minutes. Measure out ½ cup of the syrup; set aside. Pour the rest of the syrup into the prepared baking dish.

3. To make the filling, with a swivel-bladed peeler or paring knife, remove any fibrous strings from the rhubarb stems. Dice the rhubarb into ¼-inch pieces. Toss with the sugar and orange zest. Set aside.

4. To make the biscuit dough, combine the flour, sugar, baking powder, orange zest, and salt in a mixing bowl or a food processor. Mix well or process briefly to mix. Cut in the butter with two knives or by pulsing the food processor on and off, until the mixture resembles coarse crumbs. Break the egg into a measuring cup and beat slightly. Add enough milk to make ⅔ cup. Add to the flour mixture and stir with a fork or process until the dough comes together as a ball. Refrigerate the dough for 10 minutes to make it easier to handle.

5. Turn out the dough onto a lightly floured board and knead lightly 10 to 12 times. Roll out the dough to form a 9- by 12-inch rectangle. Brush the dough with the melted butter. Thoroughly drain the rhubarb (you should have about 5 cups left). Spread the rhubarb over the dough, leaving 1 inch of bare dough all the way around. Roll up the dough, as for a jelly roll, starting with the long edge. Pinch the edge of the roll to seal it.

6. Cut into 12 slices and place in the syrup, cut-side down.

7. Bake for 35 minutes. Drizzle with the reserved syrup and bake for another 10 minutes.

8. Serve warm.

12 servings

cutting butter into flour

One of the easiest and most effective ways to cut butter into flour is to grate refrigerated or frozen butter into the flour and then briefly work it in with your hands. The resulting biscuit should be very flaky.

buckles, slumps, and grunts

There is something incredibly satisfying about these old-fashioned desserts. They recall an earlier time when one couldn't run to a supermarket for a missing ingredient but had to make do with the staples on hand: flour, sugar, butter, eggs, and fruit — fresh or preserved.

This style of baking makes sense today, too. Why spend an hour shopping for ingredients to make a white chocolate mousse, when a blueberry grunt can be tossed together in 15 minutes? And the grunt may reward you with entertainment while it cooks. The blueberries simmer in a skillet under a layer of biscuit dough. As the biscuit steams, it is supposed to grunt, or sigh. That elusive sigh may happen when the fruit bubbles so vigorously that steam from the fruit levitates the biscuit, which then falls with a sigh. Nothing compares to the flavor of this simple, homey dessert.

Buckles, slumps, and grunts are almost foolproof. In fact, there is only one way to spoil a simple fruit dessert, and that is to use underripe fruit. These desserts require juicy fruits bursting with flavor. They are at their best served warm. If time is short, it is preferable to assemble the dessert, refrigerate it unbaked, and bake it right before serving.

Then there is the question of cream. A dollop of unsweetened cream is often the best topping. It cuts the sweetness of the fruit and rounds out the flavors. But no one will refuse whipped cream and vanilla ice cream if you choose to offer those instead.

5 · Puddings
& Ice Cream

Chocolate Pudding

American cooks have always been enamored of kitchen gadgets. When cornstarch manufacturers started giving away pudding molds in the nineteenth century, cornstarch sales soared and cornstarch puddings became very popular. Americans are also fond of convenience foods. Ever since Jell-O started manufacturing its pudding mix, far too few children have had the opportunity to taste creamy, flavorful, made-from-scratch cornstarch puddings, like this one.

Pudding

- 2 ounces semisweet chocolate or ⅓ cup semisweet chocolate chips
- 2 ounces unsweetened chocolate
- 2 cups milk
- ½ cup sugar
- ⅛ teaspoon salt
- 2 tablespoons cornstarch
- 2 large egg yolks, lightly beaten
- 1 tablespoon butter, at room temperature
- 1 teaspoon pure vanilla extract

Topping

- 1 cup heavy whipping cream
- 2 tablespoons sifted confectioners' sugar
- 1 tablespoon dark rum ro rum extract

1. To make the pudding, in a heavy-bottomed saucepan over very low heat, melt the semisweet and unsweetened chocolates. Stir in 1¾ cups of the milk, the sugar, and the salt. Heat almost to boiling, stirring frequently. Flecks of chocolate will remain until the pudding has finished cooking.

2. In a small bowl, combine the cornstarch with the remaining ¼ cup of milk. Add it to the hot chocolate mixture. Cook over medium heat, stirring until the mixture thickens and comes to a boil. Reduce the heat slightly and boil gently for 1 minute. Remove from the heat.

3. Gradually stir a few teaspoons of the pudding mixture into the egg yolks, mixing constantly until blended. Continue adding the pudding gradually until you have added about ½ cup. Pour the yolk mixture back into the pan, stirring until combined. Cook over low heat, stirring constantly, for 2 minutes, until the mixture is thick and smooth. Remove from the heat.

4. Stir in small bits of butter at a time and the vanilla, mixing until the butter is melted.

5. Immediately pour into six dessert dishes and cover the surface of the puddings with plastic wrap to prevent a skin from forming. Cool on a rack, then refrigerate.

6. Just before serving, make the topping. Beat the cream until soft peaks form. Add the sugar and rum and beat until stiff. Pipe a portion of whipped cream on top of each serving.

6 servings

a word about pudding

The very word *pudding* has inspired wits and pundits throughout the ages. Pudding doesn't always mean, well, pudding. If someone tells you "not a word of pudding!" then say nothing about it (late seventeenth century, early eighteenth century). "I beg your pudding!" means "I beg your pardon!" (circa 1890). "Join the Pudding Club!" (twentieth century) refers to pregnancy. A pudding-sleeves is a clergyman (eighteenth to nineteenth century); a piece of pudding is a piece of good luck (circa 1870). Shakespeare seemed to have been quite inspired by pudding, having one character threaten, "I'll let out your puddings," meaning "I'll spill your guts." And another time, "He'll yield the crow a pudding one of these days," which is a rather colorful way to talk about death.

Butterscotch Pudding

Butterscotch is a rich flavor derived from butter, brown sugar, and lemon juice. It is not clear whether there is a true connection to Scotland. The flavor first appeared in print in 1885 as *butterscot.* Ever since then it has been used for puddings, candies, and dessert sauces.

Pudding

½ cup granulated sugar

⅓ cup water

2½ cups milk

3 tablespoons butter

¾ cup firmly packed dark brown sugar

3 tablespoons cornstarch

2 tablespoons unbleached all-purpose flour

⅛ teaspoon salt

4 large egg yolks, lightly beaten

1 teaspoon pure vanilla extract

Topping

1 cup heavy whipping cream

2 tablespoons sifted confectioners' sugar

¼ teaspoon freshly grated nutmeg

1. In a small heavy-bottomed saucepan or skillet over medium heat, cook the granulated sugar without stirring until the sugar melts and is golden brown. Remove from the heat. Slowly and carefully pour in the water. (The water will steam and boil up as it hits the caramelized sugar.) Cook without stirring until the sugar dissolves in the water. Add 2 cups of the milk and heat almost to boiling. Remove from the heat and stir in the butter. Set aside.

2. In another heavy-bottomed saucepan, combine the brown sugar, cornstarch, flour, and salt. Add the remaining ½ cup milk gradually, stirring it in with a wire whisk to remove any lumps. Slowly add the hot caramel-milk mixture. Cook over medium heat, stirring, until the mixture thickens and comes to a boil. Continue stirring and boil for 1 minute. Remove from the heat.

3. Gradually stir a few teaspoons of the pudding mixture into the beaten egg yolks, mixing constantly until blended. When you have added about ½ cup, pour the yolk mixture back into the pan, stirring until combined. Cook, stirring constantly, for 2 minutes, until the mixture is thick and smooth. Remove from the heat. Stir in the vanilla.

4. Pour the pudding into six dessert dishes. Cool on a rack, then refrigerate.

5. Just before serving, make the topping. Beat the cream until stiff and add the confectioners' sugar and nutmeg. Pipe the whipped cream on top of each serving.

6 servings

Pudding is poison when it is too much boiled.

— Jonathan Swift

custard trickery

Custards can be tricky. If you take them off the heat too soon, they will never firm up. If you leave them on the heat too long or cook over too high a heat, they will curdle. How do you identify that magic moment of perfection?

First, a definition. A custard is a sweetened mixture of milk and eggs that is baked (a baked custard) or stirred on a stovetop (a stirred custard). Adding cornstarch or gelatin will help the custard stiffen.

A stirred custard should be cooked in a double boiler or a heavy-bottomed saucepan to prevent the milk from scorching and the custard from curdling. A stirred custard is done when it leaves a velvety coating on the back of a metal spoon. If you run your finger across a custard-dipped spoon, it will leave a definite track. If you have an *accurate* candy thermometer or instant-read thermometer, it will register 170°F when the custard is done.

If you are baking the custard, the baking dish should be immersed in a hot-water bath to prevent overbaking. A baked custard is done when a knife inserted halfway between the edge of the baking pan and the center of the custard comes out clean, even though the center is still jiggly. It will become firm as it cools.

Take your time with custards. Bake custards long and slow. Cook stirred custards over medium heat, stirring constantly. It should take about 10 minutes for a custard to reach the right consistency.

Creamy Rice Pudding

Rice pudding, like bread pudding, is often regarded as a way to use up leftovers. But stop right there. The creamiest, most delectable rice puddings start with short-grain or medium-grain rice, simmered to a creamy consistency in milk. The rice is then folded into a stirred custard and the result is ambrosial.

½ cup short-grain or medium-grain rice,
    such as Arborio

3¾ cups milk

    Pinch of salt

2 large eggs

½ cup sugar

½ cup raisins, plumped in hot water and
    drained

1 teaspoon pure vanilla extract

½ teaspoon ground cinnamon

    Milk, light cream, or whipped cream,
    to serve (optional)

1. In the top of a double boiler set over boiling water, combine the rice, 2¼ cups of the milk, and the salt. Simmer, covered, until the milk is mostly absorbed and the rice is tender, about 60 minutes. Stir frequently. Let cool.

2. Heat the remaining 1½ cups of milk in a heavy-bottomed saucepan until very hot but not boiling. In a small bowl, beat the eggs. Gradually stir a few teaspoons of the milk into the beaten eggs, mixing constantly until blended. When you have added about ½ cup, pour the egg mixture into the remaining hot milk. Stir in the sugar. Cook over low to medium-low heat, stirring constantly, until the custard is thick and smooth.

3. Stir the custard into the rice. Stir in the raisins, vanilla, and cinnamon until thoroughly blended.

4. Spoon the pudding into a serving bowl. Cover and refrigerate until completely cooled.

5. Serve with milk or cream passed in a pitcher or whipped cream dolloped on top (if using).

4 to 6 servings

Baked Rice Pudding

It has always been a mystery why the best-tasting rice puddings are served at diners, particularly Greek-run diners on the East Coast. But then again, diners often serve the best pies, too. What it comes down to is this: If you want good old-fashioned desserts, a good old-fashioned diner is often as good as grandmother's house.

2 egg yolks

½ cup sugar

2 teaspoons cornstarch

½ teaspoon ground cinnamon

¼ teaspoon freshly grated nutmeg

⅛ teaspoon salt

2½ cups warm milk

1 teaspoon pure vanilla extract

1½ cups cooked short- or medium-grain rice

½ cup raisins

Freshly grated nutmeg, to garnish

Milk, cream, or fresh fruit sauce, to serve

1. Preheat the oven to 325°F. Lightly butter a 1½-quart baking dish. Set it into a slightly larger pan that is at least 2 inches deep.

2. In a bowl, combine the egg yolks, sugar, cornstarch, cinnamon, nutmeg, salt, and a few table-spoons of the milk. Whisk until blended. Add the remaining milk gradually, along with the vanilla. Fold in the rice and raisins.

3. Spoon the pudding into the baking dish. Pour 1 inch of hot water around the dish.

4. Bake uncovered for 1 hour 30 minutes, stirring with a fork every 15 minutes during the first hour. This will prevent the rice from settling and will keep the custard creamy. Do not stir during the last half hour. The pudding will be done when the rice looks creamy and almost all of the milk is absorbed.

5. Remove the pudding from the water bath and let it cool on a rack.

6. Sprinkle with the nutmeg. Serve warm or cold with the milk, cream, or a fresh fruit sauce.

NOTE: The raisins can be plumped in sherry for several hours for extra flavor. Drain before using.

6 to 8 servings

Bread Pudding

This recipe is a boon to the thrifty cook.

4 slices firm white bread

1 to 2 tablespoons butter, at room temperature

½ cup raisins

2¼ cups milk, warmed

2 large eggs

⅓ cup firmly packed light brown sugar

½ teaspoon ground cinnamon

⅛ teaspoon freshly grated nutmeg

Pinch of salt

1 teaspoon pure vanilla extract

1 teaspoon granulated sugar

Whipped cream, to serve

Berries, to serve

1. Thoroughly butter an 8-inch square or round baking pan.

2. Toast the bread on both sides until lightly colored. The bread should remain soft inside. Spread butter on both sides of each slice, then cut it up into 1-inch cubes. You should have 2½ to 3 cups of bread cubes. Arrange the bread cubes in the baking pan; sprinkle with the raisins.

3. Heat the milk in a microwave or in a saucepan over low heat just until warm.

4. In a medium-sized bowl, lightly beat the eggs with a whisk. Add the brown sugar, cinnamon, nutmeg, and salt. Gradually add the warm milk and vanilla, whisking until combined. Pour the mixture over the bread cubes. Let stand for 30 minutes, pressing down the bread occasionally to absorb the mixture.

5. Preheat the oven to 325°F. Sprinkle the granulated sugar over the top of the mixture.

6. Bake for 50 to 60 minutes, until a knife inserted between the center and edge of the pan comes out clean. The pudding should be golden brown and puffed.

7. Cool on a rack.

8. Serve warm or cold with whipped cream and fresh berries.

6 servings

Persimmon Pudding

Alas, you will have to go to southern Indiana to taste this pudding made with the authentic American persimmon, a small oval fruit that is a burnt sienna in color. (Indianans call the color "persimmon color" and say there are no other words to describe it.) The persimmons you will find in the supermarket are a Japanese variety that grows well on the West Coast. These fruits are larger and less intensely flavored. Made with either variety of persimmon, this pudding summons up memories of plum pudding. It looks like a rich, dark chocolate pudding with a chewy crust but tastes light, fruity, and spicy.

1½ cups puréed ripe persimmons (3 to 4 large)

1½ teaspoons freshly squeezed lemon juice

1½ cups sifted all-purpose unbleached flour

1½ teaspoons ground cinnamon

1 teaspoon baking powder

1 teaspoon baking soda

1 teaspoon ground ginger

½ teaspoon freshly grated nutmeg

½ teaspoon salt

2 large eggs

½ cup lightly packed dark brown sugar

½ cup granulated sugar

3 tablespoons butter, melted

1 teaspoon pure vanilla extract

¾ cup milk or half-and-half

½ cup raisins

½ cup chopped walnuts

Hard Sauce (recipe follows) or whipped cream flavored with brandy, to serve

1. To prepare the persimmon purée, cut the fruit in half and scoop out the pulp with a spoon. Discard the skin, stem, and seeds. Purée the pulp in a blender or food processor, or strain through a food mill. Measure out 1½ cups and mix with the lemon juice. Set aside.

2. Preheat the oven to 350°F. Thoroughly grease and flour a 9-inch baking dish.

3. Sift together the flour, cinnamon, baking powder, baking soda, ginger, nutmeg, and salt. Set aside.

4. In a large bowl, beat the eggs until light. Beat in the brown and granulated sugars, persimmon purée, butter, and vanilla. Add the flour mixture alternately with the milk, mixing just until the batter is smooth and blended. Fold in the raisins and nuts. Spoon into the prepared pan.

5. Bake for 60 to 70 minutes, until the pudding pulls away from the sides of the pan and a knife inserted 1 inch from the edge comes out clean. The center will be a little bit soft.

6. Let cool on a rack for 5 minutes.

7. To serve, cut into squares. Serve with the refrigerated Hard Sauce or whipped cream.

6 to 8 servings

Hard Sauce

4 tablespoons butter, at room temperature

1¼ cups sifted confectioners' sugar

1 teaspoon freshly squeezed lemon juice

1 to 2 tablespoons brandy

Freshly grated nutmeg

1. In a small bowl, beat the butter until creamy. Gradually add the sugar. Add the lemon juice and 1 tablespoon of the brandy and mix until thoroughly blended and fluffy. Add more brandy, if desired.

2. Spoon the sauce into a sauce dish and sprinkle with the nutmeg. Refrigerate before serving.

About 1½ cups

palatable persimmons

What a time the early colonists must have had tasting the new foods they encountered! Take persimmons, which are plentiful in the Midwest, the Carolinas, and Virginia. In Virginia during the early 1700s, John Smith called the persimmon "one of the most palatable fruits of this land." The taste of a ripe persimmon is said to be something like a cross among a guava, mango, apricot, and tomato — very tasty in puddings and cakes. But the unripe persimmon is so acidic that it could, as one early diarist recorded, "drawe a man's mouth awrie with much torment." One must pity the poor explorer who had not yet learned the difference between the ripe and the unripe fruit.

Indian Pudding

This is one of the very oldest American desserts, taught to the colonists by the Native Americans, who called this dish *sagamite*. This version tastes faintly reminiscent of pumpkin pie, with its soft creamy texture under a glossy chestnut brown skin. The pudding will be soft when it comes out of the oven, but will firm up when refrigerated.

4 cups milk

⅓ cup yellow cornmeal

¼ cup sugar

½ teaspoon ground cinnamon

½ teaspoon ground ginger

¼ teaspoon freshly grated nutmeg

¼ teaspoon salt

½ cup dark molasses

2 tablespoons butter

1 cup light cream

Vanilla ice cream, to serve

1. Lightly butter a 1½-quart baking dish. Set it into a slightly larger pan that is at least 2 inches deep.

2. In a heavy-bottomed saucepan, heat 3 cups of the milk just to the boiling point. Mix the cornmeal with the remaining 1 cup of cold milk. With a whisk, gradually stir the cornmeal mixture into the hot milk. Cook over medium heat for 20 minutes, stirring frequently. The mixture will be slightly thickened. Remove from the heat.

3. Preheat the oven to 300°F.

4. Combine the sugar with the cinnamon, ginger, nutmeg, and salt. Add to the cornmeal mixture, along with the molasses and butter, stirring until blended.

5. Pour the mixture into the baking dish. Pour 1 inch of hot water around dish. Place on an oven rack. Carefully spoon the light cream over the top of the mixture; do not stir it in. The cream will form a skin while baking. Bake for 3 hours.

6. Transfer the baking dish to a rack for 15 minutes to allow the pudding to set.

7. Serve warm with the vanilla ice cream.

6 servings

Baked Custard

This is the ultimate in comfort food: soft, smooth, easy to digest, and just like Mom's. Baked custard certainly didn't originate in America, but it has been enjoyed here as much as it has in the Old World.

3 cups milk

4 large eggs

6 tablespoons sugar

¼ teaspoon salt

1 teaspoon pure vanilla extract

Freshly grated nutmeg

Maple syrup or sliced fresh fruit, to serve (optional)

1. Preheat the oven to 325°F.

2. Heat the milk until hot, not boiling.

3. In a bowl, lightly beat the eggs with a whisk. Stir in the sugar and salt. Add the hot milk gradually, stirring constantly. Add the vanilla. Strain.

4. Pour the filling into six custard cups or a 1-quart baking dish. Set the cups or baking dish into a shallow pan at least 2 inches deep. Sprinkle the custards with nutmeg. Pour 1 inch of hot water around the custard cups or baking dish.

5. Bake individual cups for 45 to 50 minutes; bake the large baking dish for 1 hour to 1 hour 15 minutes. The custard is done when a knife inserted near the center comes out clean. The center will still be soft.

6. Remove the custard from the hot water and place in 1 inch of cool water to stop the cooking.

7. Serve cold or at room temperature. Custard is delicious served with maple syrup or fresh fruit.

6 servings

Chocolate Mousse

Mousses originated in France but have become quite popular since the 1960s. This mousse has intense chocolate flavor.

4 ounces semisweet chocolate or ⅔ cup semisweet chocolate chips

2 ounces unsweetened chocolate

¼ cup strong brewed coffee

¼ cup plus 3 tablespoons sugar

4 large eggs, separated

⅛ teaspoon cream of tartar

Pinch of salt

1 cup heavy whipping cream

1 tablespoon brandy or 1 teaspoon vanilla extract

Whipped cream, to serve (optional)

Shaved chocolate, to garnish (optional)

1. In the top of a double boiler, combine the semisweet and unsweetened chocolates, coffee, and ¼ cup of the sugar. Place the top of the boiler over simmering water (the bottom should not touch the water). Stir until the chocolate is melted. Remove the pan from the heat and let cool for 3 minutes. Add the egg yolks, one at a time, beating thoroughly after each addition. Set aside until cool, 10 to 15 minutes.

2. Beat the egg whites until foamy. Add the cream of tartar and salt and beat until soft peaks form. Gradually add the remaining 3 tablespoons of sugar and continue beating until the egg whites are stiff but not dry. The egg whites should hold their shape and remain moist. Mix a quarter of the beaten egg whites into the chocolate mixture, just enough to lighten it. Gently fold in the remaining egg whites.

3. Beat the whipping cream until stiff. Beat in the brandy, then gently fold into the chocolate mixture. Spoon into six soufflé or dessert dishes and refrigerate until firm.

4. Serve cold with additional whipped cream and a sprinkling of chocolate shavings (if using).

NOTE: The eggs in this recipe are not cooked. Please see "Egg Information" on page 198.

6 servings

Lemon Mousse

Columbus brought the first lemon seeds to the Americas. Spanish missionaries planted them in California, where lemon crops later flourished.

1 envelope (¼ ounce) unflavored gelatin

¼ cup cold water

3 large eggs, separated

¾ cup sugar

1 tablespoon finely grated lemon zest

⅔ cup freshly squeezed lemon juice (about 4 lemons)

⅛ teaspoon cream of tartar

Pinch of salt

1 cup heavy whipping cream

1 lemon, thinly sliced

1. In a small bowl, sprinkle the gelatin over the cold water. Stir and set aside to soften.

2. In the top part of a double boiler, beat the egg yolks with a wire whisk until thick and lemon colored. Gradually add ½ cup of the sugar, beating until thoroughly blended. Mix in the lemon zest and lemon juice. Place the pan over (not in) simmering water. Cook, stirring constantly, until the mixture coats a metal spoon, about 8 minutes. Add the softened gelatin, stirring until dissolved. Place the pan in a bowl of ice water, stirring until the mixture mounds slightly when dropped from a spoon. It should be cold but not set.

3. Beat the egg whites until foamy. Add the cream of tartar and salt and beat until soft peaks form. Gradually add the remaining ¼ cup of sugar and continue beating until the egg whites are stiff but not dry. The egg whites should hold their shape and remain moist. Gently fold into the mousse mixture.

4. Whip the cream until stiff. Fold half of it into the mousse mixture. Spoon the mousse into a 1½-quart soufflé dish or eight custard cups or dessert dishes. Refrigerate until firm.

5. Pipe dollops of the remaining cream on top of each portion. Garnish with the lemon.

NOTE: The egg whites in this recipe are not cooked. Please see "Egg Information" on page 198.

8 servings

Vanilla Ice Cream

America's favorite dessert was probably invented in China and brought to Europe by Marco Polo. It was popular in the new republic; George Washington spent about $200 — a princely sum in those days — on ice cream in the summer of 1790 alone, and Thomas Jefferson is credited with bringing "French-style" ice cream made with egg yolks (like this recipe) to the United States. Dolley Madison, wife of James, popularized ice cream by serving it frequently at the White House. The ready availability of ice and the invention, in 1846, of a home-size hand-cranked ice-cream maker turned ice cream into a summer tradition. Today, each American is said to eat about 24 quarts of this frozen dessert per year, compared to about 9 quarts by each Canadian.

2 cups heavy whipping cream
2 cups milk
3 vanilla beans

8 large egg yolks
¾ cup sugar
Pinch of salt

1. In a large heavy saucepan, combine the cream and milk. With a paring knife, split the vanilla beans lengthwise. Scrape the pulp inside the beans into the milk and add the beans as well. Bring almost to a boil, then reduce the heat and simmer over low heat for 1 minute.

2. Remove the saucepan from the heat, cover, and let the mixture steep for 30 minutes.

3. In a medium-sized bowl, beat the egg yolks with a whisk. Gradually add the sugar and salt, whisking until the sugar is dissolved and the mixture is thick and lemon colored. Gradually whisk one quarter of the warm milk mixture into the egg yolks. Then slowly stir the egg yolks into the remaining milk mixture in the saucepan.

4. Cook over low heat, stirring with a metal spoon, until the mixture thickens slightly and coats the back of a spoon. Do not let the mixture come to a boil. Remove the vanilla beans.

5. Strain the mixture into a bowl, then stir a few times. Cover with plastic wrap and refrigerate. The flavors are enhanced if the mixture is refrigerated overnight.

6. Freeze in an ice-cream maker according to the manufacturer's directions.

VARIATIONS

Strawberry Ice Cream: Make the basic vanilla ice cream through step 5. While the mixture chills in the refrigerator, combine 2 cups coarsely chopped ripe strawberries with ¼ cup sugar and let stand for 30 minutes. When the vanilla mixture is thoroughly cold, stir in the strawberries and freeze in an ice-cream maker according to the manufacturer's directions.

Chocolate Ice Cream: Make the basic vanilla ice cream through step 4. Melt 2 ounces unsweetened chocolate and 3 ounces semisweet chocolate (don't use chocolate chips). Add the melted chocolate to the warm vanilla mixture and stir until combined. Strain into a bowl. Refrigerate. Freeze in an ice-cream maker according to the manufacturer's directions.

1½ quarts

Never eat more than you can lift.

— Miss Piggy

Maine Wild Blueberry Festival
P.O. Box 421
Union, ME 04862
Phone: (207) 785-3281
Web site: www.union-fair.com

National Peanut Festival
5622 Highway 231 South
Dothan, AL 36302
Phone: (334) 793-4323
Web site:
www.nationalpeanutfestival.com

Vermont Maple Festival, Inc.
P.O. Box 255
St. Albans, VT 05478
Phone: (802) 524-5800
Web site: www.vtmaplefestival.org

West Virginia Black Walnut Festival
116 Court Street
Spencer, WV 25276
Phone: (304) 927-5616
Web site: www.blackwalnutfestival.org

egg information

Eating eggs or egg whites that are not completely cooked poses the possibility of salmonella food poisoning. The risk is greater for pregnant women, the elderly and very young, and people with impaired immune systems. If you are concerned about salmonella, you can use reconstituted powdered egg whites, such as Just Whites. Pasteurized eggs, such as Davidson's, reduce the risk of salmonella food poisoning and are now available in some areas.

Metric Conversion

Unless you have finely calibrated measuring equipment, conversions between U.S. and metric measurements will be inexact. It's important to convert the measurements for all of the ingredients in a recipe to maintain the same proportions as the original.

General Formula for Metric Conversion

Ounces to grams	multiply ounces by 28.35
Grams to ounces	multiply grams by 0.035
Pounds to grams	multiply pounds by 453.5
Pounds to kilograms	multiply pounds by 0.45
Cups to liters	multiply cups by 0.24
Fahrenheit to Celsius	subtract 32 from Fahrenheit temperature, multiply by 5, then divide by 9
Celsius to Fahrenheit	multiply Celsius temperature by 9, divide by 5, then add 32

Approximate Metric Equivalents

By Weight

U.S.	METRIC	U.S.	METRIC
0.035 ounce	1 gram	10 ounces	280 grams
¼ ounce	7 grams	15 ounces	425 grams
½ ounce	14 grams	16 ounces (1 pound)	454 grams
1 ounce	28 grams	1.1 pounds	500 grams
1¼ ounces	35 grams	2.2 pounds	1 kilogram
1½ ounces	40 grams		
1¾ ounces	50 grams		
2½ ounces	70 grams		
3½ ounces	100 grams		
4 ounces	112 grams		
5 ounces	140 grams		
8 ounces	228 grams		
8¾ ounces	250 grams		

By Volume

U.S.	METRIC
1 teaspoon	5 milliliters
1 tablespoon	15 milliliters
¼ cup	60 milliliters
½ cup	120 milliliters
1 cup	230 milliliters
1¼ cups	300 milliliters
1½ cups	360 milliliters
2 cups	460 milliliters
2½ cups	600 milliliters
3 cups	700 milliliters
4 cups (1 quart)	0.95 liter
1.06 quarts	1 liter
4 quarts (1 gallon)	3.8 liters

Index

Other Storey Titles You Will Enjoy

101 Perfect Chocolate Chip Cookies, by Gwen Steege. Whether you like your chocolate chip cookies with or without nuts, chewy or crumbly, traditional, exotic, healthy, adventurous, decadent, or completely over the top, you'll find the perfect recipe in this book. 144 pages. Paperback. ISBN 1-58017-312-8.

500 Treasured Country Recipes From Martha Storey & Friends, by Martha Storey. In this chock-full-of-recipes cookbook, Martha shares her family's and friends' favorite tried-and-true country-cooking recipes. These are the simple dishes with country style that make your mouth water. 544 pages. Paperback. ISBN 1-58017-291-1.

Apple Cookbook, by Olwen Woodier. This book features unusual recipes that use North America's favorite fruit in beverages, appetizers, snacks, brunches, entrées, and desserts. 192 pages. Paperback. ISBN 1-58017-389-6.

The Classic Zucchini Cookbook, by Andrea Chesman. This completely revised and updated edition contains 225 through-the-menu recipes; an illustrated zucchini and squash primer; and information on how to select, store, clean, preserve, and substitute. 500,000 copies in print. 320 pages. Paperback. ISBN 1-58017-453-1.

Corn, by Olwen Woodier. Award-winning cookbook author Olwen Woodier celebrates this down-home, delicious, all-purpose comfort food with 140 easy-to-prepare recipes, plus information on nutrition, history, and preserving. 192 pages. Paperback. ISBN 1-58017-454-X.

Maple Syrup Cookbook, by Ken Haedrich. Maple syrup isn't just for breakfast anymore. Recipes for every meal feature maple syrup as a sweetening ingredient or flavor enhancer. 144 pages. Paperback. ISBN 1-58017-404-3.

Picnic, by DeeDee Stovel. Everyone loves picnics. DeeDee Stovel offers 29 seasonal picnic event ideas — packable repasts from an informal Berry Picking Picnic to an elegant Music Festival Picnic. More than 125 recipes for soups, entrées, salads, and desserts are included. 192 pages. Paperback. ISBN 1-58017-377-2.

These books and other Storey Books are available at your bookstore, farm store, garden center, or directly from Storey Books, 210 MASS MoCA Way, North Adams, MA 01247 or by calling 1-800-441-5700. Or visit our Web site at www.storey.com